{MIND THE}

G⬆P

{MIND THE} G⬆P

LEADING YOUR CHURCH TO AGILITY + EFFECTIVENESS IN ANY ENVIRONMENT

CLINT GRIDER

B&H
PUBLISHING
BRENTWOOD, TENNESSEE

978-1-0877-8314-7

Published by B&H Publishing Group
Brentwood, Tennessee

Dewey Decimal Classification: 253.7
Subject Heading: CHRISTIAN LEADERSHIP / PASTORAL
THEOLOGY / DISCIPLESHIP

Cover design by Tim Greene, FaceOut Studio. Map illustration by
Magicleaf/shutterstock. Author photo by Ben Miller.

1 2 3 4 5 6 • 26 25 24 23

Acknowledgments

My prayer is that this book gives pastors and ministry leaders a renewed sense of joy, clarity, and intentionality in their calling. Jesus is the hope of the world. In an ever-changing culture, never has it been more important for leaders to grow in their ability to adapt as they galvanize people toward the transformation Jesus is calling them to.

The impact of so many who have encouraged me and provided wise counsel over the years is significant. I can't begin to list them all, but would like to offer a few special acknowledgments. First, I'd like to thank several key people at Lifeway and B&H Publishing. I'm grateful for Ben Mandrell and the uncommon balance of visionary and servant leadership he demonstrates. I'd also like to thank Bill Craig, who I first met in ministry many years ago, for his thoughtful posture and gifted insight. The entire B&H team is the best of the best and has been a joy to work with. My editor, Logan Pyron, has provided especially good input that overflows from his love for people and the church.

I greatly appreciate the foundational support and important contributions of Jim Randall, Cory Hartman, and Quintin Stieff. I also want to thank core members of the Auxano team—Bryan

Rose, Mike Gammill, Kent Vincent, Greg Gibbs, David Putman, Jeff Meyer, Bob Adams, and Andrea Kandler. Your passion for the church is unparalleled.

But most of all, I want to thank my family, beginning with my precious wife, Kindra, who brings gap-minding creativity to our home and challenges me to be my best. And to my beautiful daughters, Kayln and Camryn . . . your sparkles and sprinkles are magical and reflect the love of Christ. I'm so proud of you. And to my outstanding sons-in-law . . . Carter, I love the way you approach life with both compassion and determination. And Chris, for your attention to the simple things that matter. And to my parents, Mom and Pop, your lifelong love story reflected such deep passion for each other, and a sense of joy and adventure in life even in the midst of great trials. And to my parents-in-law, Mom and Dad, for your quiet steadfastness and generous spirits. To say that God has used all of you in a major way in my life doesn't even come close to your impact.

Finally, I want to express appreciation to the many pastors and leaders who have allowed me to join them on their sometimes challenging, but always exhilarating, journeys. It's been a blessing to seek God together and see him move in extraordinary ways as he's revealed the gaps we need to mind.

Contents

CHAPTER 1

The Two Gaps: How a Pastor's Stunning Admission Revealed Every Church's Problem

I couldn't believe what the pastor had just said. Such bluntness . . . such honesty.

I hear pastors talk quite a bit. In my field, I get to interact with ministry leaders from around the country almost every day. But this leader was unusual. He had a large following and a national profile. He was a sought-after conference speaker. Author of a dozen books. Pastor of a gigachurch (the sort of church that makes megachurches look small). All in all, a model of ministry success, and a pretty modest guy to boot.

Don't misunderstand. I didn't expect him to be *dis*honest. I just didn't expect him to be *that* honest in this particular setting, at the front of a well-lit auditorium with thousands of in-person and online attenders of his church watching. And I didn't expect him to be so honest about *this*.

In the middle of his sermon, he made a startling confession about what prevents him from sleeping. "What keeps me up at night," he said, "is this question: *Are all the people who are part of this church really growing?*"

Maybe this isn't a surprise to you. Granted, there are certainly more embarrassing admissions that people make—acknowledging a lurid sin, for example. Indeed, inured to shock as we are in this generation, many people in the crowd may not have noticed what he said at all.

But I noticed it. Pastors have one main job: to grow people in Christ so they multiply the kingdom. This is essential to pastoral ministry. And yet here was this pastor, the sort of leader whom many pastors far and wide aspire to emulate, humbly admitting that he didn't know whether or not he was succeeding in the one thing he was called to do. It was remarkable.

The Root of the Problem in Church Ministry

In another way, however, it wasn't *that* remarkable, because over the years I've been hearing the same thing in different words from leaders of all kinds and sizes of churches. People call me an organizational movement expert. I focus on catalyzing momentum. I've discovered unique ways to get under the hood and help leaders discern how to adapt in a variety of conditions to achieve their church's distinct missional calling. This helps them impact the world more deeply and clearly. Along the way I've met leaders who describe different pain points to me, but their stories share a deeper theme in common.

We all say that we need to make disciples who make disciples, but we don't tell people how to get there in a way that deeply connects. Don't get me wrong; we *think* we do and we earnestly *try*. But there are many models and ideas that leaders jump to for a season, only to then jump to another. Success is limited and doesn't sustain for some reason across the whole congregation. Something is lacking.

One church leader told me, "We function like an Ivy League school, not a trade school; we impress with our theological teaching, but we aren't making practical application of the Bible in daily action the norm. We seem to have a fundamental inability to get the majority of our laypeople to the point where they start bridging divides and sharing their faith as a natural outflow of their life, especially those under the age of thirty-five. Worse, we have trouble recognizing things that we're doing ineffectively; some of our leaders even get defensive rather than addressing them."

Another church said, "We have a heart-level commitment to transforming generations of people throughout our city, but our understanding of what that means is all over the map. We've declared a model of spiritual formation stages, but despite our best intentions, it doesn't seem that people have embraced it. We have some stories of mentoring and testimonies here and there . . . but don't know whether we're actually doing it across the board with more people than the ones who were already with us."

Yet another leader shared, "In a divided world, the gospel should cut across racial, economic, and cultural barriers, but as much as we talk about it, we don't know if we're doing the right things to help our people actually live out that kind of compassion and unity. The events we sponsor seem to resonate with a lot of people at first, but then they kind of trail off and we wonder if very many are really embracing next steps that reveal the kind of confession, reconciliation, and transformation that Jesus talked about."

I could go on and on, but you get the idea. And my guess is that you can probably relate.

Perhaps you too are concerned that you don't know whether the activities of your church or network of churches are actually moving the needle in most of your people's daily lives. Or worse, maybe you *know* that you aren't moving the needle much.

Or perhaps you do know that you're making a difference—maybe even thriving in others' eyes—but you're not confident that you're making as big or widespread of an impact as you *could*. There's a drag on your effectiveness, or there's a next hill to climb and you haven't found a way to the top.

In a rapidly changing world fraught with sociocultural challenges, it feels like a struggle to figure out how to filter options and make the best decisions on what to do next.

Whatever the context—whether things could be just a little better or nothing is working at all or anywhere in between—what you're experiencing is real. It's not your imagination. And you're not alone.

I'm convinced that the root of our problem is that **there's never been a greater disconnect between God's desired outcomes, people's life journeys, and what they actually experience through church.**

Leaders broadly agree that the church is God's instrument for movement, the community God created to help people take each right next step, one after another, to grow in Christ and multiply

4

his kingdom.[1] Yet too often, despite the sincere intentions, churches struggle to deliver this in a deep, consistent way. In an age where many people already question the effectiveness of institutions, it shouldn't surprise us that "church" as an organization is viewed skeptically by some—even by some who are called to ministry.

Still, regardless of how structured or organic a person's current view of an "effective" church might be, there is undeniably more that can be achieved when a whole community of individuals is truly mobilized toward something bigger than themselves. Interestingly, as Carey Nieuwhof observes, "most of the New Testament is not about the teachings of Jesus. It's about the work of the church that Jesus initiated and ordained. . . . To pretend the church doesn't need to be organized is as logical as arguing that society shouldn't be organized."[2]

And yet, problems with this are rampant. Many churches host events that are disconnected from one another. They evaluate themselves by random anecdotes here and there or by those who participate, not by widespread production of lasting fruit. They avoid viewing their functions as an interdependent whole and neglect to improve and adapt by applying biblical principles that many other organizations find helpful. They don't always know

---

1. I realize some may disagree with nuances of this statement if it is separated from the context of this larger discussion. I do not intend to disregard constructs such as God's sovereignty, that believers *are* the church, that important sacraments are administered in church gatherings, that part of the mission is to reestablish God's kingdom "on earth as it is in heaven," etc. Many authors have written about the functions of the church, so for the purposes of this discussion I will leave that to other or future works.

2. Carey Nieuwhof, "A Response to Christians Who Are Done with Church," n.d., https://careynieuwhof.com/a-response-to-christians-who-are-done-with-church/.

how to see clearly what is happening in most of their people's lives, or how to nimbly adjust activity to escort them into their next step with God.

But this doesn't have to be the norm. Amid these challenging questions, there are leaders rising to a level of understanding and effectiveness that they didn't know was possible. They're making far better decisions in real time to help people throughout their churches grow in Christ and multiply disciple-makers in ways they never could imagine before, much less facilitate. They are no longer wondering whether they're really making a widespread difference in people's lives—they know they are.

This transformation is no miracle, but it might feel like it. Everything changes when leaders learn to mind the gap.

The First Gap: Awareness

The full significance of the phrase "mind the gap" will become apparent shortly. But first I want to point out the *two* gaps we need to mind—gaps that often frustrate church leaders' desire to grow people.

The first gap is the *awareness gap*. It's the gap between what we think is happening in people as a result of our efforts and what is *actually* happening.

Many leaders admit to truly not knowing how most people in their church are growing and struggling spiritually. They know about some, but not most. This can lead to false assumptions or misplaced hope. They recognize the awareness gap, and seek to close it with knowledge. Yet in their effort to arrive at the answer, leaders often stumble into a few attempted solutions that are very common but not very helpful.

The first common attempted solution is to count what can easily be counted: participation. The assumption is that the more people who show up or engage with us, the better we must be doing. Granted, few leaders are so unsophisticated as to take something like mere worship attendance as a sufficient indicator of spiritual maturity. Nevertheless, there are some leaders who take group participation or volunteer service as clear indicators that people are growing and living out their faith more deeply, which may not actually be so.

Unfortunately, measuring participation does not close the awareness gap, even when measuring participation in activities that are intended to help people grow. Doing so makes big assumptions about what is actually happening throughout those groups and why people are participating in them. As long as people are being socialized into more activity in the church, we're prone to give ourselves credit that they're growing, even though we don't know what that activity is producing in most people's lives.

I'm not suggesting that increased participation isn't important; I'm suggesting that many leaders stop short of examining the reasons for and outcomes of that participation.

When participation metrics become the stand-in for growth in Christ, it gradually, unconsciously shifts leaders toward a shadow mission other than the Great Commission. The subtle temptation becomes to multiply participation instead of focusing on how well that participation is training people to multiply their faith. In other words, the more that leaders equate the church apparatus with making attenders, the more zealous they will be to ram people through the system without knowing whether the system is working. And as C. S. Lewis reminds us, if the church is not making disciples, "then all the cathedrals, clergy, missions, sermons, even the Bible itself, are simply a waste of time."[3]

Even so, no leader is stuck in a *total* awareness gap; almost all leaders know what's going on in *someone's* life. Every decent leader is in touch with individuals who are evidently growing in their faith through the structures the church provides. These success stories activate the second common way that leaders ineffectively try to close the awareness gap, which I call "spotlighting."

Spotlighting is elevating a few success stories to represent what is happening among the many. When it's time to communicate

> Spotlighting is great for *communication,* but critically flawed for overall *evaluation.*

what God is doing in the life of the church, spotlighting individual stories is almost always a great move. The problem comes when leaders assume too much based on those stories. Spotlighting is great for *communication,* but critically flawed for overall *evaluation.*

The individuals you know who are growing in Christ are a real part of your church, but they aren't a random sample of the whole. Quite the contrary—these people gravitate to you (and vice versa) precisely because they are benefiting the most from the ministry. They are not average attenders of your church; they are far above average. So their testimonies do little to increase your awareness of

---

3. C. S. Lewis, *Mere Christianity* (1952 repr.; New York: HarperCollins, 2001), 199.

what is happening broadly in people's lives. We'll examine this more in chapter 2.

These inferior solutions to closing the awareness gap encourage complacency in some church leaders who are content to believe that things are "all good," especially if they are in the minority of churches presently enjoying numerical growth. Counting participants and appreciating success stories can be soothing, but they don't remove the deeper concern. Often without realizing it, leaders who don't close the awareness gap default to *leading by assumption*, a treacherous place to be. And there remains an uneasy sense that the church ought to be doing something more to make a greater impact.

> Leaders who don't close the awareness gap default to *leading by assumption*, a treacherous place to be.

Unfortunately, as long as the awareness gap exists, there is no true way to know what the "something more" ought to be. New models, interventions, initiatives, and programs are too often shots in the dark based on hunches or copying what supposedly worked for someone else, not on good information from one's own context. Aiming for improvement resembles the remark by Montgomery Scott in the movie *Star Trek*: it's "like trying to hit a bullet with a smaller bullet whilst wearing a blindfold, riding a horse."[4]

The result is whiplash—changes from the current thing to a new thing to the next thing, few of them with staying power or that build on gains of the innovation before. Paradoxically, some

---

4. *Star Trek*, directed by J. J. Abrams (Paramount Pictures, 2009).

churches are both continually changing and continually remaining stuck because they lack a clear awareness of the actual impact their varied efforts are having (or not having) on the people they serve.

The Second Gap: Connectivity

The awareness gap is one obstacle, but leaders also face a second gap: the *connectivity gap*. It's the gap between misconnected steps or ministries in your church that short-circuits their effectiveness.

Misconnection means "a wrong, faulty, or inadequate connection of things."[5]

In part, this is the gap between the variety of different things a person might engage in over time that might not feel connected to them. Some are organized church events and structures; others are personal habits like spiritual disciplines. Whether collective or individual, activities like these are intended to help people mature in Christ and live out their faith.

Unfortunately, people don't always engage in the things that might be biblically important to connecting the dots in their spiritual growth. They get stuck where they are, and all of our pleading with them to engage in missional community, or to seek reconciliation, or to dig into Scripture, or to pray, or to share their faith with others in a regular rhythm seems to fall on deaf ears. They're not connecting the dots. This is the connectivity gap in action.

All leaders encounter this frustrating phenomenon. To overcome it, some experiment with a host of tactics to persuade people to take the right next step. Others surrender to the principle that

---

5. *Oxford University Press*, Lexico.com., s.v. "misconnection," accessed 2021, https://www.lexico.com/en/definition/misconnection.

it's all in God's hands and resolve to pray more and wait longer. Most leaders typically swing between both approaches. When neither works, it is tempting to blame the people themselves for their stubbornness, worldliness, or lack of commitment.

Any of those accusations may be true (after all, everyone has a sinful nature to contend with), but the connectivity gap frequently has more to do with leaders than followers. When people don't take their next step, it's often because we haven't given them the right next step to take. From our point of view, the next step we've laid out for people makes perfect sense, yet for some reason it isn't reasonable, desirable, or feasible from *their* point of view. We introduce a new opportunity or program to engage in that feels to them like a haphazard jump with little to no relationship to what they're already doing. What looks like a step to us feels like a puzzling leap to them because it requires too many moves from where they are now on their faith journey. And whether they fully realize it or not, they've already experienced the confusion that results from jumping from thing to thing, idea to idea, preference to preference.

> People often don't take their next step because we haven't given them the right next step to take.

We aren't minding the connectivity gap when we aren't taking thoughtful, strategic action to facilitate the right next moves that respect the diversity of people's spiritual journeys.

This isn't easy to do, but it is crucial that we succeed because of the limited time at our disposal. On the church's side, leaders only have so many hours to prepare next moves for people, so the moves they present need to have a high success rate. On the people's side, they only have so much attention to give and only so many moves they can make at one time. There are many voices clamoring for their attention where they live, work, shop, give, worship, serve, and play. So in the moments that we do cut through the noise, what we offer needs to be compelling, and it needs to work. If it doesn't, people eventually tune us out.

This is the other part of the connectivity gap—not just connection between one activity and another but also *between an activity and the difference it's supposed to make in people's lives.*

This is why I assert that the root of the problem in ministry is the disconnect between God's desired outcomes, people's life journeys, and what they experience through church. When leaders don't intentionally and thoughtfully focus church ministry on *outcomes* in people's lives, it's unlikely to produce those outcomes. And leaders can't focus ministry on outcomes if those outcomes aren't clearly defined.

How Agile Leaders Mind the Gap

The oldest metro subway system in the world, the London Underground, has some stations with an unusual quirk: the platform sits against a curve in the rail line. When straight train cars line up against a curved platform, it makes wider spaces than usual between the edge of the platform and part of each car. If one of these wide spaces is right under a door, it can be a dangerous surprise for a passenger who isn't careful stepping on or off the train.

So to help passengers stay safe, an announcement booms from speakers at the stations—"MIND THE GAP"—warning people to watch out for the gap between the train and the platform. (The warning later applied to other awkward situations too, such as when trains of different heights ran through the same station, making strange vertical gaps where cars were a good bit higher or sometimes *lower* than the platform.) Today, the phrase "mind the gap" is so associated with the London Underground that it's almost a slogan, sticking in the memory of anyone who has visited that city.[6]

I love the phrase "mind the gap" because of its multiple meanings. It tells us to be careful, but it also tells us to use our *minds*. Think about phrases like "mind your manners" and "mind your mother." Minding something is more than noticing it or even recognizing it; it obligates us to do something with it.

As leaders, we must continually use our minds in vibrant new ways to evaluate and grow our effectiveness.

We need to apply the mindpower God has given us not only to the *message we state* but also the *system we make* to disciple those who believe it.

Being "transformed by the renewing of your mind" (Rom. 12:2) becomes especially significant in this context. As Tod Bolsinger points out in his book, *Canoeing the Mountains*: "In a changing world, the leader must be continually committed to ongoing personal change, to develop new capacities, to be continually transformed in ways that will enable the organization's larger transformation."[7]

---

6. Mike Horne, "Mind the Gap," Metadyne, June 16, 2013, http://www.metadyne.co.uk/mind_the_gap.htm.

7. Tod Bolsinger, *Canoeing the Mountains: Christian Leadership in Uncharted Territory* (Downers Grove, IL: InterVarsity Press, 2015), 216.

It will take all the mindpower that God grants us through his Spirit to close the awareness gap and the connectivity gap. Minding the gap in our churches, then, means more than analyzing it or talking about it or writing an article about it; it means taking active steps to close it.

Yet I use "mind the gap" for still another reason. The Underground is itself a fascinating metaphor for church ministry. What it teaches us makes some of the cloudiness of church leadership wondrously clear. The analogy of a church to a train system is the thread that ties this book together, so that is where we begin as we seek to connect people's journeys to God's outcomes again.

I use the word "journey" rather freely because they say that life is a journey. And by "they" I don't mean motivational wall-hangings or sentimental movies; I mean the books of the Bible.

The Parable of the Underground

The authors of Scripture regularly use the image of a "way" or "path" to talk about the conduct of a person's life and its basic direction, as when Psalm 139:3 says, "You search out my path . . . and are acquainted with all my ways" (ESV). It can be good or evil, as when Psalm 1 compares "the way of the righteous" to "the way of the wicked" (v. 6). Jesus himself taught that "the way is easy that leads to destruction," but "the way is hard that leads to life, and those who find it are few" (Matt. 7:13–14 ESV). The early disciples who did find it called themselves simply those "who belonged to the Way"—namely Jesus himself, who is "the way, the truth, and the life" (Acts 9:2; John 14:6).[8]

So in keeping with the picture of life as a "way" or journey, imagine a traveler making her way through a huge metropolis. In this city there are thousands of possible destinations and millions of places to stop and look around. Still, not just any place will satisfy her. What she is looking for can only be found in a few places, but she only has a vague idea of what they are and where they are. All she knows for sure is that she isn't getting very far on two feet. Not only is she lost, but even if she knew where she was going, her progress still would be slow.

As the traveler wanders through the city, she sees occasional clues to an alternate mode of transportation. Sometimes she hears a roaring, rattling sound and feels a whoosh of warm air from the grate under her feet in the sidewalk. In some places, she sees a train rolling on an elevated track passing over the street. And at certain intersections she sees a stairway plunging into a dim hole under a sign that reads UNDERGROUND.

One day she recognizes a friend going down a set of those stairs and decides to follow her. At the bottom, she learns that she has walked into something called a station, and she sees people waiting for one of those trains she sometimes sees above ground. She notices a map and begins to realize that this station is part of an entire system of stations and trains. Finally, she sees posters along the walls describing various points of interest, all of them destinations she might visit. Each one looks more amazing than the one

---

8. Leland Ryken et al., eds., *Dictionary of Biblical Imagery* (Downers Grove, IL: InterVarsity Press, 1998), s.v. "path."

before, but according to the map, these are all reachable by this underground train system.

She realizes, *This is way better than walking! Now I see the places where I want to go, and have a way to get there.*

That would be the beginning of a happy ending. But before we go there, let's rewind and tell a different story.

Imagine that the traveler descended into a different underground train system, one that's actually worse than trying to walk to some unknown destination.

Imagine that she saw trains running above ground all the time but could never find a station where she could catch one. Or that she could find a station, but the gate was locked. Or that she went down into a station, but would have to risk her life leaping across an electrified rail to get to the right platform. Or that she caught a train that the sign said was headed one way, but it was actually heading somewhere else.

Or imagine that she waits in a station for hours, but no train ever arrives. Or that she boards a train, but it starts and then stops, then starts again, then stops again. Or that the windows are stuck open and the slipstream blows debris on the passengers. Or that the doors are stuck open and people fall off the train. Or the train collides with another and gets derailed.

Or imagine that there are no places to stop for refreshment on a long journey. Or that the destinations are not as advertised. Or worst of all, that there are no destinations: the whole system is a closed loop, trains circling endlessly but going nowhere.

A traveler who encountered a train system with any of these problems, even if she were to try to make it work, would eventually give up. She would get off the train, ascend the stairs into the air outside the station, and continue her wandering on foot, no matter how useless it might be in the tangled maze of the city.

No one in their right mind would ever create a system that would cause a traveler so much frustration and even danger. But without intending it or even realizing it, churches and their leaders do so every day.

Two Critical Questions Facing Every Church

In this parable, the city is the world, the place of human habitation with its pleasures and pains, its joys and sorrows, its unity and division, its wholesomeness and pollution. The church is the Underground. Through the people who make it up, the church weaves throughout the world without the world fully recognizing it for what it is.

The purpose of the church in this parable is to help wandering people find their way to the destinations they are longing for but can't quite name and don't know how to reach. Though the ultimate destination—eternal life with Christ—is bigger than the cosmos, there are nearer but very important destinations along the way there. I call these destinations *outcomes*, personal characteristics of maturity in Christ that are revealed and grow along one's journey. These journey outcomes are larger and larger glimmers of "the prize of the upward call of God in Christ Jesus" reflected in a life being transformed (Phil. 3:14 ESV). They represent the active progress of spiritual growth and multiplication that we desire to see in all the people we serve as we equip them to be disciple-making disciples.

In their strategy to show travelers the way to these destinations, churches—from the level of an entire organization to individual followers of Jesus—fashion two kinds of helps.

The first is what I call *constants*, an individual's ongoing engagements for spiritual growth. Some constants are organized church activities like worship gatherings, groups, classes, and serving as a consistent volunteer. Other constants are personal habits or disciplines like consistent Bible reading, prayer, and regularly seeking to reconcile and help one's neighbor. Whatever the scope, constants are the trains that are intended to carry a person to destinations of Christlikeness when the person rides them over time. (Please note that my use of the metaphor, unlike the real world, assumes that a person can ride on multiple "trains" at the same time by engaging in more than one constant.)

The second way churches help travelers is with *waypoints*, one-time events or short-run experiences with the potential to lead a person into a new commitment. Waypoints are the stations that connect people to the right next constants for their journey. A waypoint might be a discipleship training opportunity or other special event inside or outside the church such as a focused community service initiative. It might be a four-week Bible study built to draw people to try out a group for the first time. A waypoint also can be a restorative ministry like counseling or group therapy—unlike other waypoints, a person may engage in that type of waypoint for quite a while, but it still isn't intended to last forever. In this analogy, all these various waypoints are the stations that inspire someone to do something new, to change their direction—to get on a train (a constant) they have never traveled on before.

To summarize, then:

- destinations = outcomes (characteristics of growing maturity)
- trains = constants (ongoing engagements)

- stations = waypoints (one-time or temporary experiences)

Here's the significance for your church:

First, every church has constants. These are ongoing activities happening week after week. But not every church's constants are delivering *perpetual movement*. Constants ought to proactively enable people to *go somewhere* in their walk with Christ. They should keep people moving forward on their journey, not stall out or go in circles by seeming like they're repeating the same thing over and over with little forward momentum. Are people motivated by your constants to stick with them long enough to experience deep spiritual transformation or do they drift away?

Second, all churches have waypoints—short-term opportunities or events—though some churches might have more than others. But not every church's waypoints become *pivotal moments* in people's lives, reaching people's hearts so they take a personal step in a new direction. Do they make sense to people where they currently are and give them a next step that is just the right distance ahead, not a leap too far? Churches without intentional waypoints expect people to hop into constants like jumping onto a moving train.

Third, most churches have not spelled out outcomes clearly enough based on their own missional context. They have a general idea of what maturity in Christ looks like—the fruit of the Spirit for example (Gal. 5:22–23)—but they have not systematically articulated what that looks like practically in life where their people live, work, and play. Journey outcomes should be *progress metrics*. Every church should seek God's wisdom in developing a relatable list of individual and shared qualities that will be nurtured on each person's journey as they engage with the church. These are the priorities, competencies, behaviors, or sensitivities that are codified as the basic aspects of following Christ in their unique missional context. These distinct outcomes should then influence the design of every part of the whole ministry system.

The Underground	What They Are	I call them . . .	They enable . . .
Trains	Ongoing engagements (personal habits, church activities that are consistent)	Constants	Perpetual movement
Stations	One-time or temporary experiences (special events, focused campaigns, restorative ministries)	Waypoints	Pivotal moments
Destinations	Characteristics of growing maturity (virtues, priorities, competencies, behaviors, relationships, sensitivities)	Outcomes	Progress metrics

Table 1: The three features of the church Underground[9]

---

9. This intends to add to the disciple-making conversation by offering new perspectives and deeper tools in areas Auxano historically referred to as measures and strategy in *Church Unique*. In its vision framing process, Auxano

Ultimately, every church has two critical questions to answer:

1. Do our stations (waypoints) connect people to our trains (constants)?
2. Do our trains take people to our intended destinations (outcomes)?

These two fundamental questions aren't meant to intimidate but to provide a glimpse of where we're going. I'm not presenting a new ministry model; I'm introducing a new way of thinking—a mentality—that transcends the din of competing models. Applying this way of thinking, depicted figuratively by the Underground, is the key to minding the awareness gap and the connectivity gap that leave churches stuck. Your leadership will grow through *responsive disciple-making* that will help you and your leaders become more and more attuned to what's really happening in the lives of

> Responsive leadership helps you and your team become more attuned to your people.

all of your people and to adapt what you're doing accordingly. In a rapidly changing world, this paradigm will help you respond flexibly to unexpected conditions and unique differences in whatever missional context you're called to.

---

originally called *outcomes* "measures." This book provides deeper ways for leaders to evaluate and adapt nimbly based on disciple-making outcomes. The terms *waypoints* and *constants* provide a new way to examine what is inside the "strategy" side of a church's vision frame (i.e., any elements of a church's current strategy can be grouped as waypoints or constants for evaluative purposes, as described later in this book).

The first step to close the awareness gap is to define outcomes (destinations), because until you name where you hope to go, you can't determine whether or not you're getting there. Until you clearly know where you want to take people, you can't get a meaningful fix on where they are today. Chapters 2 and 3 are about defining your target biblically and contextually with greater specificity than you ever have before. These chapters also explain how to accurately assess the degree to which your efforts are moving the needle to help people mature and grow in their gospel impact in these areas. You can arrive at breakthrough awareness through innovative research of what is really happening and consistent checkup loops between church staff and front-line leaders (which also works in churches where these are the same people).

Next, in chapters 4 through 8, we'll examine how to close the connectivity gap by integrating constants (trains) and waypoints (stations) into a unified whole that is greater than the sum of its parts. The careful integration of constants and waypoints—both aimed at defined outcomes—revolutionizes ministry, because it helps people who are otherwise left out and left behind to take meaningful next steps in their walk with God, one after the next. This integration will refreshingly help church staff and lay leaders clearly understand why they're doing what they're doing and how to evaluate and refine their work. Along the way I'll deconstruct common myths about church disciple-making strategies in favor of an authentically biblical paradigm that nimbly fits the changing conditions of your unique context.

Finally, chapters 9 and 10 bring it all together to illustrate how leaders can apply these principles in the day to day and year to year of ministry. I'll describe how a discipline called "moves management" from a separate but related field has surprising lessons to teach us about how staff and lay leaders can work as a more tight-knit team to make disciples who multiply and change their world. We'll also look at how the Underground paradigm can enhance your leader meetings and add new vitality and significance to the relationships between your staff, lay leaders, and congregation or network of congregations. We'll discover how leaders can mesh breakthrough awareness with wise connectivity to enable everyone in your church to gain ground in one critical aspect of spiritual growth at the same time. And we'll catch an exhilarating glimpse of how your team can experiment, learn, and experiment again, continually improving how you guide and support God's people on the path of life.

It's about People

The awareness gap and the connectivity gap aren't just problems that organizations face. People struggle with them first.

The church leaders I know got into ministry because God called them to make a difference in people's lives. They are fueled by a desire to see souls saved, brokenness healed, and people become all that God made them to be for his kingdom.

Yet when an awareness gap prevails, many of these precious people aren't truly seen, heard, and known.

And when a connectivity gap is present, they don't receive the right invitations to the right next steps that open into a transformed life.

Minding the gap, then, is an urgent and critical need. God has placed every leader in the church for this very purpose, for the sake of the people he loves.

This book shows you how to accomplish it.

CHAPTER 2

Brutal Objectivity: Obsess over Outcomes That Matter

"Something doesn't smell quite right in here." That's what Kindra, my wife, said when she walked into my home office one day. (I think I did a good job of not taking it personally.)

She noticed a very slight scent that I couldn't detect at all, but I wasn't altogether surprised. Over many years of marriage I've accepted that her olfactory prowess is superior. So I helped her try to identify the source of what I couldn't smell.

We looked and felt everywhere but couldn't find anything out of the ordinary. We were left trying to guess the most likely culprit. The simplest explanation pointed to our little, fluffy dog Belle. Belle likes to hang out with me while I work, and her crate, where we put her when we leave the house, resides in my office as well. Belle is a good officemate, and we had never had a problem with her before. She is house-trained and her crate was clean. But Belle was the easiest cause to finger and the easiest problem to fix, so that became our reigning theory. We vacuumed and cleaned the carpet, scoured the crate, and even polished the furniture. Kindra was tentatively convinced the problem was solved, so we didn't give it another thought.

Time passed until one day I got a new lamp for my office. I bent down to plug it into the socket behind the front corner of my desk, when I noticed something strange. A tiny patch of carpet in the small space between the edge of my desk and the wall was slightly but unmistakably damp. It wasn't fully wet, and there was no moisture on the wall or the baseboard—just this unusual little damp spot.

I sniffed the area and didn't detect anything (though as I mentioned earlier that didn't mean much). I reached behind the desk and carefully felt the carpet and up and down the wall and along the baseboard and it was all totally dry. So once again, I looked for the simplest explanation. I remembered my daughter had just spent some time working on the floor in the front part of my office with a big glass of water. I figured that she might have accidentally splashed a little, and the water hadn't quite dried yet. No big deal.

I wanted to be diligent about solving the problem, though, and not leave it to chance. So I set up a small fan and let it blow over the area for the rest of the afternoon. When I checked the patch of carpet again, it was dry. Problem solved.

It just so happened that several months prior to all of this, I had done another small home maintenance project. I had observed that when I got out of the shower in our bathroom, there sometimes seemed to be a little wetness on the baseboard at the corner where it intersected the shower stall. For a while I didn't think much of it, assuming that it merely got water on it when I stepped out of the stall and reached for my towel.

Eventually, however, I thought I should seal it better, so I re-caulked the joint with waterproof silicone and neatly repainted the baseboard. Things seemed fine after that.

Did I mention that our bathroom and my home office share a wall and that the shower and my desk sit against each other on opposite sides? Perhaps not—it didn't seem relevant to me when these odd phenomena were happening since they seemed to be very minor things and there was nothing on the wall or floor that appeared to connect the two.

That all changed dramatically one day when I noticed something new as I sat down at my desk. The back of the desk, just beyond my feet, goes all the way to the floor. On that day, a curvy wet band was crawling up the whole back of my desk from the floor up. We were way past damp at this point. The desk was soaked and so was the wall behind it.

We could no longer deny it. This couldn't be explained by a fluffy canine, a splash of spilled water, or abrupt exits from the shower. I didn't know what the problem was, but it was serious enough to admit that it was beyond my ability to diagnose and fix.

As it turned out, the shower pan—the layer underneath the tile that I stepped on every day—had been slowly leaking for a long time. As a result, water that didn't go down the drain had been seeping out sideways, spreading along the wall separating the bathroom from my office. A tiny bit of it occasionally emerged from the baseboard next to the shower stall. A little sometimes went under the very bottom edge of the drywall and baseboard to different isolated spots in my office on the other side. From the inside of the shower, the leak was completely invisible, but when the tile was pulled off the walls, there was mildew stretching up the drywall all the way around the base of the shower and deeply into my office wall.

The Story We Tell Ourselves

While my shower was being demolished and rebuilt, I thought about how the whole months-long saga reflected on me as a homeowner.

On the one hand, it revealed that I was meticulous and diligent about basic maintenance. If another person thought their pet that didn't smell bad before suddenly smelled a bit strange, they might give her a bath and think nothing more of it, but I deep-cleaned my whole office. If someone else saw a small damp spot on the carpet from some spilled water, they might let it air-dry on its own, but I ran a fan the rest of the day. If someone else saw a little moisture on the bathroom baseboard when they were drying off, they might ignore it, but I re-caulked and repainted the surfaces. I was in all respects a thorough and conscientious homeowner.

Yet, as thorough as I was, I was terribly lax as an evaluator. I unintentionally but repeatedly jumped to the easiest, least serious explanations of what I was seeing, even though my theories had little to no evidence to back them up. I persistently avoided the possibility that there was a deeper problem that my untrained eye's surface-level inspection couldn't detect.

In truth, I had fallen prey to mental errors called cognitive biases that had unconsciously influenced how I understood what I observed. One of these biases is called the *normalcy bias*, which is the instinctive belief that when something highly unusual (and unwelcome) happens, it isn't really happening. It's the instinct that weirdly keeps people in an unfolding disaster, such as a building with smoke alarms going off, from fleeing the scene as quickly as they can. The instinct also triggers in the middle of the night when your spouse asks, "What was that noise?" and you reply, "I'm sure it's nothing, honey."[1]

The other mental error I was committing is the well-known *confirmation bias*, in which a person weighs what they see and hear according to what they want to believe. Without realizing it, they maximize evidence that confirms their opinion, and they minimize evidence that contradicts it.[2]

The truth is, unconsciously I didn't want to believe that anything out of the ordinary or expensive to fix was happening in my house. Neither an unusual scent nor dampness in multiple adjoining rooms were enough to dislodge my bias. They *were* enough to stimulate me to flurries of conscientious action, but they weren't enough to make me admit my ignorance or accept an unpleasant truth. It finally took the undeniable presence of a soaked desk panel and wall to overturn my firm assumption that everything was under control.

I would feel worse about this, but I know I'm not alone. These mental errors are extremely common to the human race—including church leaders.

---

1. Amanda Ripley, "How to Get Out Alive," *Time*, April 25, 2005, http://content.time.com/time/magazine/article/0,9171,1053663-1,00.html.

2. Shahram Heshmat, "What Is Confirmation Bias?" *Psychology Today*, April 23, 2015, https://www.psychologytoday.com/us/blog/science-choice/201504/what-is-confirmation-bias.

Is it possible that your evaluation of your church is not as accurate as you think?

We are all afflicted with confirmation bias. We apply unconscious assumptions about what we already believe to the myriads of people we see from the platform—many as opaque as the wall behind my desk if we're honest—and propose a theory to make sense of what we're seeing.

Some church leaders have a bias toward optimism; they're inclined to see things as rosier than they actually are when they observe their church. If participant numbers are going up, a leader who leans toward optimism might say, "Things are good! God is blessing us!" even if they have no idea whether or not the whole crowd is actually becoming more Christlike. If their positive outlook is called into question, they may spotlight a few individual success stories of conversion and spiritual growth to validate their bias.

We should remember, however, that spotlighting is inherently misleading because success stories alone are never a representative sample of the whole. It's like an advertisement that shows people who lost a hundred pounds on a diet plan, but in tiny print at the bottom of the screen are the words "results not typical."

A thought-experiment bears this out. Imagine that every Sunday for a year, you put a different person on the platform to share how their life has been changed through the ministry of your church. The cumulative weight of all these testimonies would leave a powerful impression that amazing things are happening in the church—and in the lives of the testifiers, they truly would be. But if your church has five hundred in weekend attendance, the year of testimonies would highlight barely more than 10 percent of the body (and if your people only attend twice a month on average, the testimonies would only highlight 5 percent of the total). In other words, for a year, it might appear that the next Great Awakening was breaking out in your church, yet based on what you actually know, nine of ten could be totally untouched by it.

Are you evaluating your church's effectiveness by the 10 percent who are testifying to a changed life or by the 90 percent who aren't?

Other church leaders have a bias toward skepticism; they have a basic doubt that they can really know what's going on in people. So even if numbers are rising some, they can't shake the concern that things aren't what they seem, and spotlighted success stories, while appreciated, offer little lasting comfort given the larger concern.

Skepticism, however, is no solution when doubt isn't based on any more evidence than the optimist's hope is. Even if skeptical leaders are right that things aren't as solid as they appear, *why* are they right? Skeptical leaders rarely take the next step to investigate below the surface to see what's really going on. That might be the case because they don't know how, but it also might be because it seems more spiritual and orthodox to say, "Only God knows the human heart," shrug, and leave it at that.

> Are you evaluating your church's effectiveness by the 10 percent who are testifying to a changed life or by the 90 percent who aren't?

Whether we lean toward optimism or skepticism or swing back and forth between the two, it's easy to explain our observations with a story that fits our expectations. If things are going well, it's because

God is moving or because we're committed to ministry excellence or because we're warm and friendly or because we're faithful to the gospel. If things aren't going well, it's because of the competition of youth sports or because people prioritize other things during the summer or because the younger (or older) generation isn't committed or because our volunteers aren't willing to do enough.

So, in general, when good things happen, we think it has to do with the leaders (though some of us are quick to say "to God alone be glory" for what's happening). When we aren't seeing the results we want, we think it has to do with the followers. This is an important example of *the fundamental attribution error,* which describes how, due to our biases, we have an erroneous "tendency to attribute another's actions to their character . . . while attributing [our own] behavior to external situational factors outside of [our] control."[3]

Depending on our disposition, we might focus our casual evaluation optimistically on the 10 percent who testify to a changing life or skeptically on the 90 percent who don't. But either way, we rarely know why we see what we see. All we have are some general figures and a few anecdotes. While those data are better than nothing, it's all too easy to spin them into a tale to explain what's happening with as little evidence to support it as my flimsy theories about the smell in my office and the water on my carpet.

Notice that what I was seeing in my house appeared to be discrete phenomena happening at widely separated times. So I came up with separate ideas of what caused a faint smell here, a

---

3. Patrick Healy, "The Fundamental Attribution Error: What It Is and How to Avoid It," Harvard Business School Online, June 8, 2017, https://online.hbs.edu/blog/post/the-fundamental-attribution-error.

damp spot there, and a bit of moisture in another room. In reality, though, all these phenomena were connected, because they were all aspects of a single system. Seeing separate problems as having separate causes is the natural way that most of us think, because it's the easiest way to think. But that doesn't make it the right way to think. Our churches are much more complex, integrated systems than my shower stall—whatever you see happening in one place, good or bad, is almost guaranteed to be related to someone or something else that at first seems totally unrelated. But unless you do real evaluation at a deeper level—going behind the walls and under the tile—you'll never see it.

So, I want to propose a different way to evaluate. I believe it's possible to know what is happening in the spiritual lives of the whole breadth of the people in your church to a much greater extent than you've ever experienced before. You can go from making guesses about why things look as they do, motivated by your unconscious biases, to actually knowing what's really going on systemically behind the wall of your ministry. In other words, you can close the awareness gap. Most importantly, once you know where people really are spiritually, you can then do something about it to move people to their next step.

I'm talking about leaders shifting from counting heads to checkup loops and from spotlighting the few to truly seeing the many. In the next chapter I get into the nitty-gritty of how this is done. But that's not step one. First we need to talk about ministry evaluation itself—not the method of it but the very notion of it.

Why We Don't Evaluate Ministry

All of us are always evaluating without trying. It's hardwired into human brains to take in data from the world around them and tell a story that explains what they see. I didn't have to do anything special to notice water on my floor or to invent the explanation of a spilled glass of water. And you don't have to do anything special to notice how full the room is on a Sunday morning to come up with a reason for why it's more or less full than you thought it would be. We all do this instinctively.

In this basic sense, evaluation is not unusual or controversial. But when I talk with church leaders about evaluation, many of them are skeptical; something in them resists the idea. Again, I'm not proposing that we start evaluating for the first time in our careers. We can't start doing something we've been doing all along. I am, however, proposing that we evaluate ministry efforts *differently* and more thoughtfully than most leaders have ever done before. This raises fear in some leaders' minds, which I want to explore.

Fear #1: Evaluation Puts God in a Box

When I talk about evaluating spiritual health and growth, some leaders respond that it isn't just impossible; it's wrong. Many claim that it is an unfaithful attempt to confine God, who sovereignly moves in different ways in people's lives. God can do anything, and he resists human systems to predict or manage him. Creating spiritual health criteria and a system for checking on them puts God in a box.

What is the heart of this objection?

First, let's acknowledge that it's a strong statement of resistance. In our day, the phrase "don't put God in a box" is quoted with weighty reverence as if it were a Bible verse, though it doesn't actually appear in the Bible. It's the sort of statement that closes off conversation rather than opening it up. When someone tells you not to put God in a box, they're essentially telling you that the topic is not up for further discussion.

To be fair, the statement does speak to a biblical truth that God frequently defies human expectations. He confounds the wisdom of the wise. He surprises people with plans they never imagined. His ways are greater than our ways, and his thoughts are higher than our thoughts.

But is this the only way that the Bible describes God—that he's so unpredictable, keeping us so off-balance that he's virtually a force of chaos, shifting and changing constantly?

To the contrary, the unpredictability of God is perfectly balanced in Scripture by the predictability of God. He is faithful; his character doesn't change. He's kept the seasons revolving since Noah. He's the author of the laws of the universe. He's not the God of disorder but of peace. He inspired sages to write proverbs and issue instructions that teach that certain actions have reliable consequences.

A full picture of God in Scripture affirms that we can't keep God in a box we build, but God usually works through boxes or patterns that he himself builds. The problem isn't the box; the problem is which box we're focusing on. Due to our biases, we like to build boxes ourselves and paradoxically tell others that if they don't fit into our box, they're putting God in one. However, as Trevin Wax notes, "If there is a God and he really did make you and the rest of the world, then you don't get to define him in relation to you; he gets to define you in relation to him."[4]

None of this should intimidate us from trying to evaluate spiritual growth. Instead, it should motivate us to evaluate spiritual growth according to God's design. It challenges us to define criteria of spiritual health that fits what God has revealed by his Word. It stimulates us to understand nuances of the fruit of the Spirit well enough to recognize it when we go looking for it.

For certain, God sometimes defies the norm. But he can only defy the norm if there's a norm to defy. God will cause a plant to grow up in one day for Jonah while allowing countless plants to grow on the normal timetable he designed. God will bring an occasional Saul of Tarsus to growth in Christ in a wholly unexpected way, but meanwhile there are countless believers proceeding to Christlikeness by a regular pattern despite intricate variations in each life.

If we're honest, this is how we handle virtually everything else in ministry. Most of us don't walk into weekend worship unsure whether we're going to do the basic things we did the week before— singing, praying, preaching, and so on—because we say we can't put God in a box. To the contrary, we follow a regular pattern while remaining open to God changing the plans.

All leaders know this. So to be candid, when leaders push back against a deeper approach to evaluation by saying they don't want to put God in a box, there's probably something else going on.

---

4. Trevin Wax, *Rethink Your Self: The Power of Looking Up Before Looking In* (Nashville: B&H Publishing Group, 2020).

Fear #2: Evaluation Will Take a Lot of Work

In his book, *Every Good Endeavor,* Tim Keller talks about how God has given us innate desires for work: "When we work, we want to make an impact. . . . Nothing is more satisfying than a sense that through our work we have accomplished some lasting achievement."[5]

For some leaders, when they think about defining and evaluating God's desired outcomes for people in their church, they fixate on the work that it might take to get there. Figuring out how to devise non-legalistic tools that could actually measure outcomes, learning what a checkup loop is, and deciding how to establish one for a reliable flow of information from all parts of the church feels overwhelming to them. It seems like a huge effort—if it's even possible—and they feel like they're swamped with work already.

So let's start there, with all of the work you're currently doing. How do you want to spend your time?

When I detected problems in my office and bathroom, I put a lot of time and effort into addressing them. As it turns out, my effort was ineffective and ultimately pointless, even though I thought I was doing the right things. If I had just called a plumber—which would have taken a small fraction of the time I used to clean my office from top to bottom and to caulk and paint the bathroom baseboard—I would have used my time much better.

The same is true in ministry. You're going to spend a lot of time working and serving no matter what you do. Yet, as the quote attributed to Peter Drucker says, "There is nothing so useless as

---

5. Tim Keller, *Every Good Endeavor: Connecting Your Work to God's Work* (New York: Penguin, 2012), 101–2.

doing efficiently that which should not be done at all."[6] So you could continue spending time as you're doing now, conscientiously keeping everything running and starting new initiatives with no real idea whether what you're spending time on is actually working as effectively as it could, if at all. Or you could take some of that time to close the awareness gap so that your *informed* effort moves the needle in people's lives in a more widespread, more impactful way than ever before.

Yes, regularly evaluating the spiritual condition of your congregation with thoughtfulness and sophistication comes at a cost. But so does *not* doing so. You pay a far greater cost of years' worth of opportunities for many people to take their next steps with Christ that didn't happen because no one helped them figure out where they really were and what their best next step could be.[7] The cost of evaluation isn't a tax; it's an investment, and the return on that investment is extremely high.

> The cost of evaluation isn't a tax; it's an investment, and the return on that investment is extremely high.

Fear #3: Evaluation Will Get Us in Trouble with People

When I talk to some leaders about evaluation, their minds immediately focus on how people in their church might respond— and how those reactions might recoil back on the leaders.

---

6. https://www.brainyquote.com/quotes/peter_drucker_105338
7. This observation is related to the concept of opportunity cost, defined by the *Oxford English Dictionary* as "the loss of potential gain from other alternatives when one alternative is chosen."

One knee-jerk response from some leaders is "judge not, lest ye be judged." There is a legitimate concern beneath this overreaction. We don't want to give the impression that salvation comes by works. Works-based falsehoods leave many people in despair, exclusion, isolation, and dishonesty, and others in ceaseless labor and spiritual pride.

Of course evaluation must be set in the context of the gospel of grace. Moreover—and crucially—it must not be cast as leaders' examination of people but rather as believers' spiritually empowered examination of themselves in the spirit of 2 Corinthians 13:5 ("Test yourselves to see if you are in the faith. Examine yourselves") and Psalm 139:23 ("Search me, God, and know my heart; test me and know my concerns"). As Dane Ortlund reminds us in his book, *Gentle and Lowly*, "when the Bible speaks of the heart, whether Old Testament or New, it is not speaking of our emotional life only but of the central animating center of all we do."[8]

Keeping this in mind, I'll explain how to do evaluation in a context of spiritual growth and grace in the next chapter. But first, we need to answer a question pointed at ourselves: Are we concerned about not judging people for their sake or for ours? Is the greater concern that our people will take issue with us for making them feel judged?

That concern is linked to another one—not so much about the results of any one investigation as about the consequences of instilling a leadership culture that looks for results. If leadership goes down that road, they might discover that a certain ministry strategy or program is not producing as much fruit as it could and should.

---

8. Dane Ortlund, *Gently and Lowly* (Wheaton, IL: Crossway, 2020), 18.

Thoughtful leaders probably already have a hunch about the current state of some of these strategies, but once they get empirical data, it's harder to ignore the reality. Then they'll be faced with the dilemma of what to do about it. If they don't do anything, they'll continue pumping energy into something that doesn't do as much as it should to advance God's mission. But if they try to improve it, they risk the wrath of volunteers and participants who are devoted to the way that it is. As long as leaders play "see no evil" and avoid evaluating activity for results, they irrationally think they can keep themselves out of a bind.

Other leaders see the risk of evaluation tending the other way—not toward eliminating what people like but toward binding themselves to give people more of what they want. I remember one lead pastor of a large church who initially fought against the idea of an organized, systematic approach to hear from people. In his long experience, every time the congregation was ever asked about anything in a survey, he only succeeded in harvesting a laundry list of opinions and consumeristic cravings. It pinned leadership to the wall to make everyone happy and reinforced the worst possible message to church attenders: church is *All About You.*

Don't worry: that kind of survey is the *last* thing I have in mind when I talk about defining and evaluating outcomes of spiritual growth in people's lives and closing the awareness gap. But before I demonstrate the difference, I want to observe what these "people" concerns have in common: they are all based in fear of how people will react to leaders and what they will demand of them.

There's no avoiding it: acquiring brutal objectivity about what we're doing in the church exposes the degree of fear we have of the people we serve. I assure you that objective evaluation *done right* does not have to create an adversarial situation—in fact, it creates unity, freedom, and momentum that people will ultimately thank you for! When leaders resist the idea, it raises the awkward question of whether we avoid evaluating people's spiritual growth and church effectiveness not because of how it supposedly harms them, but because of how it might unsettle us.

Fear #4: Evaluation Might Make Me Look Bad

Probably the deepest, most genuine reason that leaders resist evaluating people's spiritual health and church effectiveness is that they're afraid of what their discoveries will say about them as leaders. Leaders want to feel successful and—consciously or subconsciously—work hard to come up with reasons to demonstrate and justify that success.

- As long as evaluation is dominated by head count, then the well-attended things I'm running proclaim that I'm doing a good job.
- As long as evaluation is dominated by spotlighting, then the semi-isolated success stories I share will proclaim that all is well. But take those away, and who knows what I'll find— maybe nothing.
- Maybe I'll look stupid, because something I should have been aware of is now on display for everyone to see.
- Maybe I'll look incompetent, because that thing that I said we had to do to be successful is actually ineffective.

- Ministries might get cut. Maybe I'll lose my job.
- What if I can't live with my own inadequacy?

These fears that threaten to rise over our heads and drown us feel real when we give ourselves permission to feel them, and they unconsciously drive us to avoid accountability when we try to smother them. So it's critical that you know the truth.

The truth is that the enemy uses these fears to bind you to ignorance, because he wants to keep you as ineffective for the kingdom as possible.

The truth is that avoiding evaluation leads churches to confuse busyness with progress and attending church with growing in Christ.

The truth is that avoiding evaluation allows churches to justify programs that are past their prime and makes it difficult to stop doing anything to start doing something better.

The truth is that avoiding evaluation allows leaders to justify hectic inaction, a life of doing ministry activity hither and yon without doing much that's deeply productive at all.

The truth is that in any discipline, especially one in which people's lives lie in someone else's hands, action without evaluation is malpractice. In ministry it is spiritual malpractice.

The truth is that God has called you to more than this. He has given you a job to do because he totally accepts you, not the other way around. He didn't call you to mere activity; he chose you to bear fruit that will last (John 15:16). Don't be afraid to dig more deeply than you ever have before, because Jesus promised that when you know the truth, it won't bind you; it will set you free (John 8:32).

The Joy of Becoming a Mad Scientist

Obsessively defining and evaluating by outcomes that matter—the destinations of growth God has for your people—yields five concurrent benefits that don't happen to this degree in any other way.

1. **Evaluation invigorates culture.** Naming the character qualities and journey expressions we want to exhibit as a community of disciples raises the bar in catalyzing a more widespread, intentional culture of growth in following Jesus. But the defined list becomes a dead letter if our activities don't actually help people live that out.

Consistently evaluating the deeper impact of what we do as a church communicates our seriousness. It gives us clear and vibrant ways to train and mobilize our staff, lay leaders, and entire congregation. It builds an agile, life-giving culture of research, experimentation, and development. It demonstrates that we're aligned and committed to growing disciples for gospel impact. And it reinforces that we're passionate about doing it in increasingly effective ways *together*.

2. **Evaluation inspires volunteers.** I once was listening to a church's student ministry team that was afraid of burning out its volunteers. The staff would seek leaders for weekly student small groups in the fall. Then they worked to sign up host families for a big winter discipleship weekend. Then, they recruited group leaders again for the spring, then helpers for a follow-up spring retreat, then for a big summer camp, and once again for the next ministry cycle in the fall. Each time the team would go back to many of the same volunteers and ask them to pitch in. It seemed exhausting for everybody.

The solution wasn't to ask the volunteers to do less but to commit to something bigger—to change from recruiting volunteers to this or that program, one at a time, to recruiting them to the whole mission of that ministry year round. The leader team could make that shift because the church had recently defined its journey outcomes. So before the next fall ministry season, they didn't say, "We're looking for fall group leaders." Instead they said, "We're looking for people yearning to see these outcomes in teenagers' lives over the next year." They began recruiting people not to an activity at a time but to a mission together, not to a vehicle but to a destination.

The difference is huge. Recruiting people to a mission aimed at clearly defined outcomes increases people's passion for what they do. It actually makes them eager for evaluation, because they want to see success and want to change their approach if they're not getting it. It makes them willing to sign up for multiple lay leader and volunteer roles well in advance because they see how doing so fits into the big picture. It makes them more flexible about methods because they haven't signed onto a method but to a mission. And it decreases how often they need to be asked for help, because they've already made a bigger commitment; they're up for anything.

> Recruiting people to a mission with clear outcomes increases their passion for it.

3. **Evaluation quiets complaints.** This doesn't mean that it necessarily makes people complain less (though that often does happen eventually due to greater mutual understanding). I mean that people's complaints that seem more about misaligned

preferences than the disciple-making purposes of the church carry less weight. It also provides leaders clear and gracious language to use in responding.

To clarify, evaluation does not justify an overconfident attitude that says, "Here's what we've decided to do, we're not changing, and if you don't like it you can go somewhere else." When evaluation is done right, it breaks down that attitude by making church leaders much more thoughtful and sensitive to the possibility that they haven't made perfect, be-all, end-all plans. Instead, they understand frequent course corrections are needed. They're affirming and living out another maxim attributed to Drucker: "Knowledge has to be improved, challenged, and increased constantly or it vanishes."[9]

What I am saying is that evaluation done well provides a better basis for course corrections than reactions to mere hunches, whining, or squeaky wheels. Leaders can humbly decline to pursue every change that people *want* because they are rigorously pursuing every change that people *need*, and they have reliable investigative evidence to validate that they can see the difference.

4. **Evaluation relieves pressure.** When evaluation is humbly and carefully—but decisively—introduced by a lead pastor, it actually can take pressure off of leaders.

"This is essential for kingdom innovation," as Doug Paul describes, "because this very spiritual process only becomes possible when we start to remove our pride and self-belief from the equation. *You* can't make kingdom innovation happen . . . without the work of the Holy Spirit."[10] Still, we as leaders often add pressure

---

9. https://www.brainyquote.com/quotes/peter_drucker_154448

10. Doug Paul, *Ready or Not: Kingdom Innovation for a Brave New World* (n.p., 100 Movements, 2020), 60.

when we behave as if the evaluation we're doing depends on our talent and level of perceived success versus our bold faithfulness to the specific kind of shepherding God is actually calling us to.

One time I sat across the desk from a women's ministry leader in a large urban church. Every women's ministry leader would probably say that her mission is to make disciples, but this leader was unusually self-aware. She admitted to me that her functional mission—her *real* role description, as evidenced by the expectations she felt—was to find the next, greatest guest speaker for the next big event and the best video Bible study to attract the most women each spring and fall.

But then she told me how everything changed for her when the church redefined ministry growth targets based on clear discipleship outcomes, not mere activity or participation. "It takes an unbelievable amount of pressure off," she said. Evaluation—*real* evaluation—didn't make her feel confined. She was liberated. Using ways of thinking outlined in the rest of this book, she felt free to experiment and explore. She was free to ideate with other church leaders to discover new ways to help women grow in their faith based on *where they actually were* in relation to the desired journey outcomes for their lives. She could do so without being chained to the same programs and the same, supreme measuring stick of attendance growth. She discovered that focusing on the right outcomes bore fruit that was much greater than just numerical growth.

The delight I saw in this ministry leader is what I hope to see in every church leader. Don't you think God wants that kind of undergirding joy that transcends the challenges of ministry for every leader he calls to equip his people? I believe he does. And I believe it can happen too. That leads us to the last benefit.

5. **Evaluation energizes leaders.** It energizes them to be who they're called to be.

In West Orange, New Jersey, you can visit the huge laboratory complex of Thomas Edison's varied companies, which today is a unit of the National Park Service. You can walk through machine shops, the world's first recording studio, a jaw-droppingly beautiful library, and showcases of the many inventions that erupted from Edison's geyser of team innovation.

But one stop on the tour is a narrow, low building a good deal smaller than the main edifice. It was the company's chemistry lab, which is actually where the inventor of the phonograph and per-fecter of the light bulb spent most of his time. Every day of the year, the temperature in the chemistry lab exceeded one hundred degrees Fahrenheit. There was one small fan, positioned just above Edison's desk. But chemists in three-piece suits would go to work in that stiflingly hot room for hours every day without complaint, because they understood the privilege of being one of the members of a team achieving the most advanced technological breakthroughs in the world.

Edison was famous for trying, testing, failing, and trying again, hundreds of times. He was astonishingly cheerful about it, *because his tests weren't random—one test's results bridged to the next as they continued focusing on intentional, precise outcomes.* It is said that he viewed every experiment as a success, because at the very least he would have discovered what did *not* work, which no one had ever known before.

There's no reason that church leaders can't have the same joy. As Nieuwhof says, "The key to seeing transformation take root is to keep changing, keep experimenting, keep risking."[11]

Every team with clear evaluation methods can become a gang of mad scientists, happily tinkering away, exploring, investigating, adjusting, trying, learning, and trying again, all the while doing better and better at helping *everyone* in their church to grow in their journeys with Christ.

In the end, that's what evaluation is for.

---

11. Carey Nieuwhof, *Didn't See It Coming: Overcoming the Seven Greatest Challenges That No One Expects and Everyone Experiences* (Colorado Springs: WaterBrook, 2018), 110.

CHAPTER 3

Outcomes 101: How to Create Progress Metrics for Present Action

For generations, one of the most common conversations was to ask for or to give driving directions. It was a normal and often required part of daily life. Today though, I can't recall the last time I've had a conversation about directions. GPS devices have almost entirely filled the need. For the first time in history, we have technology that plots your location on a map and tells you exactly where you are and can guide you to where you need to go.

"Where you are," however, can have more than one meaning. "Where you are" only means something relative to where something else is—a town, a road, a street corner, a gas station. Those are the kinds of features you immediately see when you open up a map on your device. Right away you know where you are in relation to the world in general: "I'm in Smithville on Highway 28 at the corner of Maple Street, where a 7-Eleven convenience store is."

In one respect this is a rich amount of information. But in another, it doesn't reveal much at all. If you only plot your location, it tells you something about your present, but it doesn't connect it to your past or your future. It doesn't tell you where you've been or where you're going. It doesn't tell you how far you've come, how far you have yet to go, and what direction you have to head to get there.

It isn't until you add a second location to the map—namely, your intended destination—that you grasp where you are in a deeper, fuller way. Once you add a friend's address to your map, you gain a completely different set of information: "I'm 37 miles northwest of Jim's house, and it will take me 50 minutes to get there." Without a defined destination, you don't know where you are relative to where you want to go, and you have no help getting there.

Acknowledging this reality is important if we are to live out Bolsinger's definition of *leadership*: "energizing a community of people toward their own transformation in order to accomplish a shared mission in the face of a changing world."[1] To lead well, we must make clear the individual and shared destinations we are seeking *as well as* where we and our people are on the journey toward them.

> Get clear on your shared destinations and where your people are on the journey.

In the previous chapter, I made the case that evaluation is essential for ministry, yet leaders often neglect it and even avoid it. I maintained

1. Tod Bolsinger, *Canoeing the Mountains: Christian Leadership in Uncharted Territory* (Downers Grove, IL: InterVarsity Press, 2015), 42.

that church leaders can't excel at their mission or truly help people unless they measure the results of their work by something much deeper than common metrics like attendance. I warned against the all-too-common danger of relying on spotlighted success stories, because they are not adequate indicators of the church's impact on most people's lives.

In this chapter, I want to go a step further. Here we will examine how to define destinations that uniquely fit the culture and calling of your church—the various outcomes along people's life journeys that we pray will emerge and grow in the discipleship process—because if you don't name where your people are going, you can't locate where they are in relation to their destination. Then, I will illustrate how to close the awareness gap about where your people are in their progress toward these destinations with an engaging, relational tool called the Mind the Gap Survey. By that point we'll get an early look at how the information gathered from good evaluation can help leaders facilitate deeper, widespread breakthrough in people's lives.

Start by Defining Your Church's Outcomes

In the illustration of the Underground introduced in chapter 1, travelers' destinations represent the "outcomes" in their lives or more descriptively "journey outcomes." Journey outcomes are personal characteristics of a growing maturity in Christ that a church has named in light of its unique calling in God's greater story. Let's discuss the four parts of this definition.[2]

---

2. Will Mancini has called outcomes "measures" and "missional marks." Mancini, *Church Unique: How Missional Leaders Cast Vision, Capture Culture, and Create Movement* (San Francisco: Jossey-Bass, 2008), 151–63.

1. Journey outcomes are *personal characteristics*. Outcomes are not defined in terms of the organization's growth but in terms of the personal growth of the people the organization serves. (Organizational metrics like participation aren't what we're talking about here.) People are the important thing, the primary target. Outcomes represent steps toward the destinations where individuals are headed in their journeys with God—namely, emerging competencies, perspectives, sensitivities, and actions that will characterize their lives as the Spirit applies his word to their hearts and as they engage more deeply in the shared mission of the church.[3] As such, a common and helpful technique to help people relate to them is to phrase them in the first person.

2. Journey outcomes characterize *a growing maturity in Christ*. They paint the picture of a person who is being formed by God into the likeness of Christ. The full suite of your outcomes, taken together, should touch all parts of a person's life. They are the result of the Holy Spirit transforming a person's life as a gracious gift from God. They don't describe a person's life in a perfect, resurrected state; they describe what a winding journey of growing maturity and intentionality looks like in this present age as we grow into completeness bit by bit (compare 2 Pet. 1:3–8[4]). As a result, out-

---

3. The relationship between organizational metrics and journey outcomes resembles the relationship between lead measures and lag measures, respectively, as described in Chris McChesney, Sean Covey, and Jim Huling, *The 4 Disciplines of Execution: Achieving Your Wildly Important Goals* (New York: Free Press, 2012). Increasing attendance in ministries is a valuable goal, for example, but only if what happens there results in journey outcome growth in people's lives.

4. "His divine power has given us everything required for life and godliness through the knowledge of him who called us by his own glory and goodness. By these he has given us very great and precious promises, so that through

comes are relevant to every believer at every maturity level; they should stretch us both in our relationship with God and in our relationship with others whether we've been following Christ for sixty days or sixty years. It is especially important for outcomes to reflect a growing missional lifestyle based on the shared vision of the church—so they don't just describe being a good person, or knowing the Bible and spending time with God in prayer, for example, but also personally and contextually living out one's faith as a disciple maker.

3. Journey outcomes are characteristics that *a church has named*. They must be explicitly stated and defined, and the statements must be made by your church. They can't be left to a vague understanding, and articulation can't be put off onto someone else. They must be phrased in a relatable way that makes sense to your people using culturally relevant language, understanding that people will be at different points on their journeys. It takes work to name and prioritize outcomes without trending toward broad religious terms that may be commonly referenced but not commonly understood. Your church's list of named outcomes also should be concise enough to be usable and not overwhelm. They should represent the things your church is committed to as most important for your congregation to consistently interact on. (I'll explain later in this chapter how to go into more detail *within* each of your journey outcomes,

---

them you may share in the divine nature, escaping the corruption that is in the world because of evil desire. For this very reason, make every effort to supplement your faith with goodness, goodness with knowledge, knowledge with self-control, self-control with endurance, endurance with godliness, godliness with brotherly affection, and brotherly affection with love. For if you possess these qualities in increasing measure, they will keep you from being useless or unfruitful in the knowledge of our Lord Jesus Christ."

but for now, focus on a fairly concise list of the most important things.)

4. Journey outcomes are characteristics that a church names *in light of its unique calling in God's greater story*. Note that there are multiple places in the Bible where characteristics of Christlikeness are listed—from the two great commandments in Matthew 22 to the qualities of love in 1 Corinthians 13 to the fruit of the Spirit in Galatians 5, and on and on. These statements are all complementary with one another, but each of them also can stand on its own. Each one is a fresh articulation of the goal of maturity in Christ that will be lived out differently for each believer based on the unique situations they face on their journeys. There also likely will be unique aspects of a person's involvement in your church's specific context or vision that you deem important to include in your outcomes. As mentioned earlier, I encourage you to include several that reflect disciple-making characteristics based on your distinct culture. In *The Trellis and the Vine*, Colin Marshall and Tony Payne discuss the importance of this call for every believer and remind us that "despite the almost limitless number of contexts in which it might happen, what happens is the same: a Christian brings a truth from God's word to someone else, praying that God would make that word bear fruit through the inward working of his Spirit."[5] As we'll discuss more later, including culturally-specific disciple-making marks in your outcomes will allow you to better create the conditions that grow them in your context. Just as the Bible itself doesn't contain just one articulation of outcomes for every setting,

---

5. Colin Marshall and Tony Payne, *The Trellis and the Vine: The Ministry Mind-Shift That Changes Everything* (Youngstown, OH: Matthias Media, 2009), 39.

there isn't just one articulation for all churches. Your church has the opportunity to draw on biblical wisdom to craft your own summary of what Christlikeness looks like according to the specific passions for God's kingdom that he has uniquely implanted in your church. As Neil Cole describes, "What is most important is that you listen to the Lord in your own missional context and follow His lead. You will not be disappointed if you do that."[6]

Accordingly, I have no interest in telling anyone what the ideal priority of characteristics of a mature disciple should be. I also don't want anyone to copy another church's outcomes, because I would hate for that to short-circuit the power that comes from defining their own for themselves based on their church's unique DNA and kingdom calling. Still, I wish to give a few examples as sources of inspiration for other church teams doing their own work.

The church examples below frame their journey outcomes in the form of questions that a disciple can ask themselves and reflect on. This is not the only way to state outcomes, but it's been very useful to the churches I have served and the Jesus-followers who belong to them. The beauty of a question format is that it can capture the essence of each outcome idea while still giving room for people to apply it based on where they are and the Spirit's movement in their life. The questions together can serve as a modern version of the self-examination questions that saints of previous eras like John Wesley and Jonathan Edwards used to ask themselves daily in their time with God. I've even known of individuals in these churches to use them as a spiritual discipline the same way.

---

6. Neil Cole, *Church 3.0: Upgrades for the Future of the Church* (San Francisco: Jossey-Bass, 2010), 93.

They cohere with David's attitude when he prayed, "Search me, God, and know my heart" (Ps. 139:23).

For instance, one influential church in a small city frames its outcomes in the form of seven Life-Changing Questions:

- How am I listening to God today?
- How does my last decision reflect that God owns everything?
- Who am I leading to their next step with Jesus Christ?
- How am I engaging other generations and cultures?
- Who am I allowing to honestly know me?
- How am I partnering with [church name] to help people change the world?
- How am I living today like Christ is coming back tomorrow?

A church with a deep liturgical tradition also uses seven questions for its outcomes, but they are linked up with creative role titles for a follower of Christ:

- Kingdom Seeker: How am I seeing God and his grace in my life?
- Need Meter: How do my neighbors experience God's love as I serve them?
- Story Teller: When am I telling God's story by sharing mine?
- Iron Sharpener: Who is growing alongside me as I grow?

- Truth Lover: How is daily repentance and forgiveness transforming my relationships?
- Joyful Giver: How does my generosity fuel God's work?
- Obedient Follower: How is the Holy Spirit leading me to follow Jesus?

A multi-ethnic church in a high-tech corridor also uses roles to define its destinations. In that church's case, however, each role is a heading under which to bundle several questions in a four-by-four structure:

- Beloved
  — How am I delighting in God through personal and corporate worship this week?
  — How am I confessing my challenges with sin this week and experiencing his forgiveness?
  — How am I experiencing increasing security in Christ by praying and listening to God?
  — How am I creating more margin and rhythm in my life for rest and renewal?
- Truth-Bearer
  — How am I falling more deeply in love with the reading and obeying of God's Word?
  — How is God's Word shaping the way I think, feel, and act this week?
  — How am I encouraging someone with God's Word this week?

— How am I committing to others in the regular study of God's Word?

- Teammate
  — How am I growing in serving others out of joy in response to God's grace?
  — How am I teaming up with my small group and church for training and accountability?
  — How am I persevering through inconvenience to more deeply serve and equip others?
  — How am I deepening my friendships by being more vulnerable to know and be known by others?

- Bridge-Builder
  — How am I stretching myself to better engage the unchurched with the gospel?
  — How am I more deeply connecting with other generations and cultures in Christ?
  — How am I pursuing reconciliation within my family, church, and other relationships?
  — How am I prioritizing time to help someone grow in their love for God and others?

A diverse urban church in a large city also groups outcomes by category, in its case according to the disciple's purpose:

- My purpose from God
  — How am I knowing and loving Jesus better today than yesterday?

- — How am I discovering and developing my unique, God-given purpose?
- — How am I listening and responding to the Holy Spirit throughout my day?
- My purpose in the church
  - — How am I being real and accountable in a small group of disciples?
  - — How am I applying what I'm learning in training experiences?
  - — How am I giving and serving joyfully in my church?
- My purpose in the world
  - — How am I living out my God-given purpose where I live, work, and play?
  - — How am I sharing the gospel with people who don't know Jesus?
  - — How am I serving the hurting and broken here and around the world?

You might already use questions like these in your ministry. I know of churches that sometimes share or project a reflection question like these at the end of sermons. What sets these examples apart, however, is that churches have named them as the top questions of their body. A person's growth in the way they engage with Christ and others while continually integrating these ideas into their daily lives represents a powerful movement. Over time, they get asked and discussed repeatedly in a variety of ways in every setting from the big group to smaller groups to one on one. They get asked at every age level (tweaked sometimes for children). They pervade the entire system of the church. These questions don't cover every single virtue or practice or circumstance; there's always room for more questions. But these questions have been made the top priorities by the church based on the leadership's belief that the Holy Spirit will escort any person from one of them to whatever area in their life he wants them to see.

Going Deeper to Make Your Outcomes Measurable

I love journey outcomes like the examples above. I find them inspiring, and the people who identify with these churches do too. People have an innate desire to become something more and to be part of something greater. Christ redeems that impulse from proud, egotistical ambition into yearning for his kingdom, glory, and goodness. Articulating destinations in a way that recognizes the progression of the journey helps church leaders put that yearning into captivating, motivating words.

Left in this form, however, there is still something missing. In general, these journey outcomes are difficult to measure on their own. There's no mile marker or scale for "Kingdom Seeker" or "my purpose in the world." Unless some tangible, realistic, more definitive proxies stand in their place, leaders can't evaluate where their people are spiritually and whether the church's initiatives are helping them make progress.

In addition, the people of a church themselves need something more concrete. By nature, journey-based outcomes are broad principles that develop differently over time. As a result, left on their own, they can be vague enough that optimists can too easily rationalize how they're true of their lives if they don't have something more objective and specific to dig into. On the other hand, pessimists or pragmatists can feel defeated by outcomes that might seem lofty to them. They might aspire to become a Truth Bearer or an Obedient Follower, but the goal seems far away. They won't reach it perfectly before Jesus returns, so how do they know they're faithfully growing and making progress that is Christ-centered? What handholds can they grip along the way?

The next step, then, is for a church to tie each outcome to what I call *outcome expressions*. These expressions are subpoints of each outcome that are more concrete and recognizable than the outcome alone.[7] Outcome expressions come in three basic forms.

1. *Foundational discipline.* This is a habitual practice that keeps a believer conversing with God and that nourishes their spiritual health and dependence on him.

> Outcome expressions explain what it means to live out each outcome personally.

We can see an illustration of this by looking closer at the outcome example from a church above that asks, "How am I listening to God today?" One foundational discipline the church ties to this outcome is, "I set aside time daily to study and meditate on Scripture." Another is, "I go to the Bible to find answers before I go to other sources." These two discipline examples are *expressions* of listening to God. By comparing their life to statements like these, a person can become more intentional and make ongoing progress toward the intended destination.

---

7. For example, a church with six journey outcomes might have four or five more concrete expressions ("I" statements) associated with each one. Meanwhile, the church above with sixteen outcomes might choose to build just two more specific expressions for each of the sixteen.

2. *Spiritual sensitivity.* This is a person's recognition that something is present in their soul or in their relationship with God that wasn't there before.

The church's journey outcome, "How does my last decision reflect that God owns everything?" is detailed by several spiritual sensitivities. One is, "I find great joy in obeying God's direction for my life." Another is, "I want to seek and be a part of whatever God is up to." The church is intentional about shepherding and equipping people in these sensitivities so they become a more and more frequent expression of each person's daily walk with Christ. Once again, these expressions bring greater specificity to the stated outcome on people's journeys.

3. *Missional intentionality.* This is an expression of a person's life that shows they are actively seeking to bring God to others and others to God as part of the church's shared mission.

In this church's example, a number of expressions tied to, "Who am I leading to their next step with Jesus Christ?" are missional intentionalities. One is, "I have shared the gospel with someone in the past month." Another is, "I regularly disciple or mentor someone I can name." They have several more. Missional intentionalities like these describe concrete indicators of progress toward the church's broader destination of regularly connecting with others to make ever-growing disciples.

Again, each church's outcome expressions will (and should!) be different from these. Whatever combination of missional intentionalities, spiritual sensitivities, and foundational disciplines a church chooses to define must be shaped by their distinct culture, context, and calling. A leader's commitment to define and measure them at that level of detail has everything to do with whether their church achieves true breakthrough.

Churches' Most Common Measurement Mistake

Before we discuss how to measure progress to destinations practically, it is critical to understand what is *not* a good expression for journey outcomes. To be specific, do not use frequency of attendance in church activities to help you measure outcomes. *This is the number-one mistake churches make when they begin defining outcomes.*[8]

For example, if your church defines a journey outcome as "worshipping God," do not use regular attendance at a worship gathering as a stand-in for it. If you have an outcome called "deepening relationships," do not use attendance frequency in a small group as a stand-in for it. If you have an outcome called "knowing my purpose," don't use completion of a new members' class as a stand-in for it.

> Do not use frequency of attendance to measure outcomes.

This warning might puzzle some leaders. It's quite common to count participants in activities like these. In fact, if any measuring is happening in a church at all, participation is usually the thing

---

8. Willow Creek uncovered this common mistake when it conducted its in-depth study called Reveal. When it measured the equivalent of journey outcomes and participation in church activities as separate variables for the first time, it discovered that how much church activity the most devoted disciples participated in had no influence on whether they continued growing spiritually. Greg L. Hawkins and Cally Parkinson, *Move: What 1,000 Churches Reveal about Spiritual Growth* (Grand Rapids: Zondervan, 2011), 16–18.

measured. So what's wrong with using participation in church activities to indicate progress toward journey outcomes? What's wrong with measuring whether a person worships God by how often they attend a worship gathering?

Let me illustrate from a place where I spend a lot of time: the airport. I fly a lot for my job and have access to the lounge of my preferred airline. I've come to appreciate not only the peace and quiet inside, but also the refreshments. One of the common offerings available at breakfast time is hard-boiled eggs. I enjoy hard-boiled eggs, and usually plan to get some before my morning flight out. Unfortunately, I learned early on that the lounge was consistently failing to boil the eggs properly. When an egg is boiled right, the shell flakes right off, but this egg's shell seemed to be superglued onto the egg white. The first time it happened I tried to break my way in, but all I succeeded in doing was pulverizing the shell and yanking off chunks of egg along with it. At first, I thought it might have just been a bad batch, until the same thing happened over the next several visits. There was a time I even saw a guy trying to pry the egg open with a knife. He didn't get any further than I did.

One day, I decided to be part of the solution. I graciously walked up to the person keeping the refreshment bar stocked. I started with a compliment and then with a smile began a friendly conversation about the eggs. I pleasantly showed her the problem, sought her sympathy, and expostulated on a great technique for boiling eggs that might help the person in the kitchen. After staring at me for a second, she smiled and said, "Okay, thanks so much for letting us know," which was her polite way of telling me that she just wanted to get on with her shift.

A good part of a year went by, and the eggs still hadn't improved, even after a few more gracious attempts with a manager or two. I finally gave up.

I try to imagine the mindset of the person boiling the eggs. I figure it must go something like this: "When I got this job, I was told to boil eggs. I was told to follow a procedure to boil the eggs. I think I did my best to follow that procedure. Therefore, I did my job to make hard-boiled eggs."

What's the issue? It's that *adhering to a process doesn't guarantee quality if it doesn't result in the desired outcome.* Just because you follow a series of steps accurately doesn't mean that the result is any good. A genuine quality control test for a hard-boiled egg isn't a process *adherence* question: "Did the cook boil thirty eggs in the large metal pot for 15 minutes?" It's a results question: "Is the egg fresh, cooked well, and can I peel it?"

The difference is crucial, because if your quality control question is about whether you followed a particular process, the process itself is never challenged. The process might have serious issues, but you'll never know it until you judge it by what the process is producing. W. Edwards Deming famously claimed that at least 85 percent of bad outcomes can be attributed to flaws in the system, not mistakes by workers.[9] I wasn't blaming the cook for the bad eggs; I blame the process the cook used to make them. Something had to change in order to produce peelable eggs.

It's easy to see how silly, bizarre, and frustrating it would be to count inedible eggs as a good outcome just because you followed the recipe that produced them. But isn't that how things

---

9. Mary Walton, *The Deming Management Method* (New York: Berkley, 1986), 94.

often go in churches? Church leaders have a recipe for producing good Christians: it's called worship services, groups, serving, and membership, or some variation of these. It's common for church leaders to call people good eggs by the activities they attend. But that assumes that the worship services, groups, volunteer opportunities, and new member's class are actually working as intended to help people grow in Christ and make disciples over the course of their individual journeys. The results of that ministry process are the very things that need to be evaluated to determine whether something might need to be improved.

On the flip side, when someone is not fully participating in the church's mission and activities, it's easy to finger the person themselves as the cause. It's easy to say, "If *they* were more committed, they would grow in Christ and engage more deeply with us." But that lets the process off the hook. Although it may be true that spiritual immaturity, worldliness, or even outright rebellion is preventing a person from greater engagement, it is also quite likely that the system (or process) is to blame. There may be good reasons why a rational, well-intentioned believer might not engage in church activities or initiatives the way they are currently arranged. The problem might be in the system, and to paraphrase Deming, the system is the responsibility of leaders, not participants.[10]

By contrast, when you keep the destinations of maturity in Christ distinct from the system of trains and stations that get them there, insights emerge that you would never gain otherwise.

For instance, imagine hypothetically that your church has defined a journey outcome that a disciple of Jesus "deepens

---

10. Walton, 94. In the context that Deming operated in, he maintained that oversight of the *system* is the responsibility of management, not workers.

relationships with other believers through encouragement and accountability" (and you of course also defined what that means in your context with concrete outcome expressions). If you found that, in general, people who are consistently living that out also are part of a certain type of small group at your church, you'd likely think those types of small groups might be helping people deepen relationships in the way you've defined. But you can't automatically make that conclusion. Perhaps those groups attracted people who already were doing well in those areas. Still, this does reveal there might be a *potential* correlation that you could then investigate further to try to understand what the relationship is between the outcome and the activity. (You can do this with a checkup loop, which I'll describe later.)

Let's say after a verification process that you find the training in all of your small groups really *is* helping people deepen relationships through encouragement and accountability, but only 30 percent of your church's regular attenders are in a small group. Your next step might be investigating what is keeping the other 70 percent from being part of them and then changing the system to overcome the obstacles.

Now, imagine instead that you discover that small groups *don't* appear to have a consistent impact on whether people deepen relationships in the way you've defined. Maybe they're not doing accountability well; they're mainly just study or social groups. Or maybe they're doing okay in some of your defined expectations but not others. Or maybe they're all over the map. Then you'd have a very different problem to investigate and solve—why the church's small groups do not seem to consistently foster deeper relationships any better than anything else in life.

Notice that these are entirely different problems that probably have quite different solutions. Knowing the difference keeps leaders from wasting time trying to fix the wrong thing. *But you can never get this kind of deep, thoughtful understanding of your church as long as you use participation as your main measuring stick.* Instead, look deeply within your entire church for progress of people's growth in foundational disciplines, spiritual sensitivities, and missional intentionalities (the clearly defined *expressions* of your journey outcomes), and use *that* to assess the effectiveness of what you're doing.

The Power of Asking the Right Questions the Right Way

Once a church defines its outcomes and the more detailed expressions that exhibit them, leaders can get a baseline on the present state of the congregation with a confidential and anonymous Mind the Gap Survey. As Jim Randall, cofounder of Auxano, has said: "Many pastors struggle to discern between what they hope their people believe about disciple-making and what those people actually live out." The Mind the Gap Survey is a tool that closes the awareness gap regarding people's challenges and how to address where they need help to grow. It also helps leaders identify connectivity gaps where church waypoints and constants aren't integrated with one another well—or in terms of the Underground, where stations and trains aren't linked to get people to their destinations. With insight from this outcome expression-based survey, leaders can make the right adjustments to lead people to the right destinations from where they are right now. As I'll describe more later, you can create one on your own or with help.

The survey is a combination of two elements. First, most of the survey questions are tied directly to the church's outcome expressions. The survey measures these by confidentially asking for the respondent's current rhythm in living each of them out. For instance, if a church has a journey outcome of "moving close to God each day," one expression of that outcome might be, "I set aside time daily to study and meditate on Scripture" (notice that's an example of a foundational discipline). Another expression might be, "I find myself briefly praying many times throughout the day to seek God's direction" (a spiritual sensitivity). Yet another might be, "I intentionally watch for the movement of God around me so I can see and join him in what he's doing" (a combination of spiritual sensitivity and missional intentionality). The survey asks the person if each expression *currently* reflects their rhythm never, rarely, sometimes, often, or always. Their responses to five or so expressions like these track their progress toward the one journey outcome (destination) of "moving close to God each day." The survey continues in the same manner with the church's other journey outcomes and expressions.

Second, other Mind the Gap Survey questions provide background information on the person responding to them. This includes demographics like age, gender, and marital status. Churches also often include questions about the person's relationship and involvement with the church—how long they've been part of the church, their relationship with Christ, their engagement with various groups, whether they volunteer, and so on. These all are customized to fit the culture, organization, and language of each church.

The combination of background information and progress toward destinations is extraordinarily powerful. The intersection of the two enables leaders to see exactly where spiritual strengths and weaknesses are in different parts of the congregation more clearly than what instinct, speculation, or spotlighting can provide. They can see how length of time at the church, engagement rhythms, types of connection, and other factors may be influencing (or not influencing) specific groups of people inside the church in different ways. It helps leaders know how to focus and shepherd the *whole* church in a more complete way than ever before.

It's worth mentioning that there are a number of spiritual health index tools out there that you can get off the shelf and deploy in your church. The problem is that those tools measure your church against their own outcomes or research interests, not yours. The journey outcomes of the churches I've described in this chapter didn't come off the shelf—they are made from scratch and taste like the unique churches that made them. Homemade outcomes are the best kind, because the churches that make them own them deeply. In the same way, the best survey for your church is the one that reveals people's progress toward the outcome expressions that *you* have defined. It isn't to compare your church with any other one, only to compare it to what you believe God wants each person to become using your language in your context.

Before I show you a real-life example of a Mind the Gap Survey in action, here are a few bits of advice on the practicalities of creating and administering one.

I want to stress that any church can do this if leaders work at it together. There also are multiple easy delivery options, from pen and paper to free online tools, some of which are quite sophisticated. So no church is completely limited—if you do it, you will learn a lot! That said, however, the expertise of an experienced *Mind the Gap* facilitator like those at Auxano goes a long way. It's an art to write a series of good outcome expressions that are clearly understood by the respondent, get at precisely what you want to know without overlapping other questions, and don't slant the answer with built-in bias. Then on the back end, it takes some strong social-scientific statistical skills to analyze the data to bring out the most meaningful connections. So consider getting the help of a seasoned navigator to give you a hand.

My other advice is to consider conducting the survey as part of worship services in a season with typically strong attendance. I say this not because it's the most practical but because believe it or not, taking the survey can and should be a deeply moving and impactful experience. It's extremely important to cultivate the right mindset and heart right before taking the survey so people are profoundly honest about where they are on their faith journey right now.

Churches often start the gathering with songs about God searching our hearts, cleansing us, and showing us the way followed by a sermon on being open and honest with God. Ideally, the sermon would be the culmination of a series where you've covered the biblical principles behind your church's journey outcomes over several weeks and have encouraged your people to be present this week. As your sermon transitions into the application point of taking the survey as a congregation, take it in your hand and graciously walk through the sections of the survey, describing how the process will work. As you do this, the most important part is to find and read aloud a particular outcome expression (or two) and say something like: "I used to do this. I've done this before. I have good intentions of doing it, but the truth is, I'm not doing it at all right now. So I'll mark 'never.'" Modeling that kind of transparency gives everyone permission to be really honest and to provide the most accurate data possible, limiting the so-called "halo effect" of respondents saying they're at a better point than they actually are (or responding how they think a "good Christian" should). Let your people know that it's okay for many responses to be "rarely" or "never" if those are accurate. It's confidential and anonymous and the important thing is to be fully transparent about where you are with each question right *now* in your life.

Most importantly, in introducing the survey, the pastor has a chance to cast the entire experience not as a works-based judgment from a God who is grading us on our performance but as a grace-based moment of intimacy between each person and their loving Father in heaven, celebrating every step of progress and encouraging every step to come. As John Calvin writes, "Nearly all wisdom we possess, that is to say true and sound wisdom, consists of two parts: the knowledge of God and of ourselves."[11] In that hushed, holy, prayerful time of reflection with the survey, God reveals both. He may change people's lives before leaders have even gotten a single answer back!

How an Honest Church Learned They Weren't Being Honest with Each Other

To take a practical look at these principles in action, let's look at one community-focused church in a midsized metropolitan area

---

11. John Calvin, *Institutes of the Christian Religion*, 1.35.

that created a Mind the Gap Survey and a bit of what they learned from it.

Leading up to the survey, the church preached on their seven journey outcomes, including definitions and biblical principles for each. One of their outcomes focuses on how each person is engaging with "key relationships" in their life, and is stated this way: "How are my key relationships healthy and honoring to God?" To help each person's reflection, the church's survey asked about their personal rhythm in living out five expressions that make that one broad outcome more concrete. Two examples are "I am known for making decisions with integrity and keeping my word" and "Those closest to me view me as a joyful and encouraging person." (By the way, those two outcome expressions could be a form of missional intentionalities, because they reflect starting points of how a person engages with others to share aspects of their faith.) I want to demonstrate how data from this single journey outcome reveals a complex, nuanced picture that significantly closed leaders' awareness gap and set up practical changes the church could make to help people grow in Christ.

First, leaders learned some very good news about the church. This outcome about healthy, God-honoring relationships is one of the church's strongest. A majority—sometimes a large majority—answered "always" or "often" to all five outcome expressions associated with it, which was worth celebrating! The expression about integrity got especially high marks; an amazing 92 percent of attenders and 96 percent of members said they are often or always known for making decisions with integrity and keeping their word.

On the other hand, although people's key relationships seemed good on the whole, there was a weak spot: only 52 percent said that they were often or always open and transparent about sharing their fears and struggles with a few Christian friends. So what was going on? Why would nearly everyone be known for integrity in their key relationships but only half would be known for vulnerability in their relationships?

Drilling deeper into the survey results provided clues to the answer while also raising more intriguing questions. For instance, leaders saw that even 84 percent of newcomers (people who had attended the church for less than two years) thought they were generally known for integrity. This puts the integrity score in a different light. Was the church doing much to help people live with integrity, or was it instead attracting people who were *already* living with integrity?

Peering into the data further, leaders noticed other interesting connection points. They saw that two-thirds of senior respondents opened up to their close Christian friends about their fears and struggles, but only one third of respondents in their forties did. In addition, women were more likely to be open with their friends than men. The gender difference wasn't that surprising to leaders based on their personal experience in that church, but the significant generational or life stage difference was surprising. Anecdotally, people in their forties seemed to be as involved in life groups and other church activities where leaders thought a culture of openness was the norm. Why then were older attenders displaying more vulnerability in relationships than middle-aged attenders? Why was the equipping in that area not working as well as it could?

Putting the data together, people in this church seemed to be confident that their light was shining in some ways to people around them, but a number from certain demographic groups were more hesitant to reveal the struggles in their lives to other Christians. This sparked helpful questions among church leaders. Are some people in the church "known for" their integrity because they don't open up about the times when they *don't* act with integrity? What roadblocks prevent people from openly sharing their fears and struggles with Christian friends? How can we as leaders clear those roadblocks and replace them with on-ramps?

Another correlation was that two thirds of respondents who attended a life group or served in the church four times a month reported that they often or always shared about their weaknesses with Christian friends. It wasn't surprising, but it was reassuring to find that people in regular personal touch with other believers in the church were more likely to open up about their lives. What wasn't clear was the direction of influence. In other words, did participating in church activities lead people to open up with other believers, or were people who were already inclined to open up naturally gravitating to church activities while more closed people stayed away? Questions like these provided pastors with specific ways to engage with their on-the-ground lay leaders to find the answers and to do something about it. (I'll give specifics on how to do this in the coming chapters.)

As this church's Mind the Gap Survey shows, once leaders knew what they were looking for and crafted an instrument to find it, they could see ministry realities that they never knew existed. If they wondered about something before, it was only anecdotal which was insufficient to help them investigate more deeply where people were getting stuck. Also keep in mind that this example only looks at part of *one journey outcome of a seven-outcome survey (with forty-three outcome expressions).* It is just a fraction of the insight the church's leaders gleaned from defining their destinations and asking people about their progress. And it doesn't illustrate how multiple outcomes influence each other and paint an even broader, richer, and deeper picture, which I'll give more examples of later.

Again, this is an example from just one church, but I've seen breakthrough understanding come in many other churches whose leaders learned things like:

> "We're successfully getting the idea across that the church exists to equip people to reach others, but we're not providing people with the on-ramps they need to actually do it."

> "When we do short-term city projects, we get a big turnout and great photos, but most of our people aren't serving others in a regular way even though we thought they were."

> "We're an ethnically diverse church, but in their personal lives, people aren't crossing cultural lines to tell others about Jesus."

> "We say we're committed to transformational compassion and reconciliation, but most of our people aren't living it even though we thought we'd trained them."

Still, the survey is just the first step to closing the awareness gap. In the example I discussed, the survey raised important questions that church leaders didn't yet have answers to. Leaders had a vastly better grasp of *what* was happening, but they were still in the dark about *why* it was happening other than speculation. And without knowing why, they didn't know how to best respond to help their people grow spiritually.

To answer those crucial questions, they needed another key tool to close the awareness gap: what I call a Checkup Loop. As a key part of responsive leadership, this relational tool is a continual conversation between a staff leader and their circle of frontline lay leaders on *defined topics and questions* that emerge from the data you're seeing. This goes beyond those lay leaders who help run your ministries. I'm talking about equipping groups of people with ways to get a deeper understanding of *why* certain things are happening (or not) in people's lives and whether the church's current approaches are making a difference. The checkup loop launches from the survey to acquire actionable intelligence to help leaders adapt and guide their church with responsive nimbleness.

In that sense, the survey provides *baseline awareness* and the checkup loop provides *ongoing awareness.* Both are needed for leaders to consistently mind the awareness gap.

> Mind the Gap surveys tell you *what* is happening. Checkup loops tell you *why.*

When leaders do so, they then can address the connectivity gaps among the things people experience in church and the destinations God has for them. They gain the understanding to design an ever-improving, flexible, potent system to help people get where God wants them to go.

I describe what the checkup loop is and how to set it up in much more detail in chapter 9. But before we can make the most of a checkup loop, we have to pause our exploration of evaluation to take a long look at the word I just used: *system.* It is no easy topic.

I've found that some pastors long to construct a rational system in their church to make and grow disciples. Meanwhile, other pastors are deeply skeptical of anything to do with systems, believing them to be vain, man-made attempts to do what only God does in people's hearts. In the next chapter, I want to make the case that systemic thinking is both biblical and essential—but also that God's kind of system is like nothing most people expect.

{ CHAPTER 4 }

The Factory Fallacy: Why Pastors Love (and Hate) Systems for the Wrong Reasons

On a late Sunday afternoon I found a seat at a round table in the back of a large, air-conditioned meeting room in a spacious church building. Happy conversations of hundreds of people filled the air with a buzz of energy. These were the most engaged core leaders from ministries across the church, and they had come to learn about an exciting new church initiative.

Worship songs and a funny skit boosted the mood and warmed up the crowd for the lead pastor. Taking the stage, he introduced the purpose of the gathering, expressing his sincere appreciation for everyone who came. It was a great start, and people were eager to learn about the new venture.

That's when the pastor asked a question that unexpectedly brought the lively atmosphere crashing down: "Hey, would someone please call out a point that I made in my sermon this morning?"

Crickets. No one said a word.

Five seconds passed, then ten. Still silence. You could feel the discomfort.

Fifteen seconds. Twenty. The pastor still didn't say a thing. He was just staring at the leaders with a slight grin. He didn't even restate the question. The silence was becoming awkward.

Twenty-five seconds. Thirty. It felt like an eternity had passed. You could hear a pin drop. This was a well-liked pastor and strong teacher at a prominent *Bible* church, mind you, where preaching of the Word is a big priority. Yet none of the core leaders of the church could remember what was said in services they attended that very morning.

Finally, someone took a risk and spoke up. "You were sharing something about . . ." The pastor took the person's vague remembrance of a tangential remark and steered it to reiterate one of the sermon's main points. He then quickly and mercifully moved on and the tension in the room began to ease, but only slightly.

He then asked a new question: "What's our mission?" Immediately a woman shouted out the answer with a few others following right behind her.

"What are our core convictions?" Bang, bang, bang—voices called out in rapid succession. Everyone started breathing easier; these were things they knew.

"What are the outcomes we're looking for in a disciple's life journey?" Again the leaders swiftly responded with precision.

Then the pastor brought his point home. "Don't worry about not being able to restate part of my sermon," he said. "I didn't expect you to entirely—but good grief, I didn't think it would be *that* bad!" Everyone laughed and the room relaxed. But then he revealed something deeper.

"You heard something only one time, and I asked you to spit it back to me. Even if you understood it, even if you appreciated it at the time, it's no small thing for your brain to absorb it and say it back in your own words later." He continued, "But I also suspected that you'd have no trouble telling me our mission, core convictions, and discipleship outcomes, because you've heard them over and over again. We build them into everything we do—what we say at meetings, what we talk about one-on-one and over social media, even what we have hanging on the walls and projected on the screens."

"I didn't expect you to recall what you learned from my sermon. I did expect you to recall what you learned from our system."

What Keeps Leaders with the Best Intentions from Being Intentional

Dallas Willard defines *discipleship* as a process to "bring Jesus' people into obedience and abundance [fullness of life in Christ] through training," which he claims never happens without "a serious and expectant intention."[1] I imagine every reader would basically agree with this idea. But as is typical for Willard, each word of his sentence is loaded with a meaning that may not be obvious at

---

1. Dallas Willard, *The Divine Conspiracy: Rediscovering Our Hidden Life in God* (New York: HarperCollins, 1998), 315.

first. It begins to disturb us when we go deeper and take inventory of how our ministry efforts actually demonstrate our "serious and expectant intention" to make disciples.

I once spoke with a pastor who was frustrated because a lay leader didn't seem to embrace an important principle that the pastor was trying to establish in the church's culture. "I just don't understand," he stammered. "I preached this six months ago. Back then the person seemed totally on board. He even came up to me and talked with me about it afterward. What happened?"

Around the same time I heard another pastor say, "At some point you have to stop being spoon-fed an interpretation of the Bible by someone else. You have to begin interpreting the Bible yourself. We cut up food for a toddler, we teach a ten-year-old to cut up her own food, and we expect an adult to cut her food herself."

I agreed with what the pastor was saying. But the irony was not lost on me that he said it while preaching his sermon from a platform on a Sunday morning—an event that every week consumes immense resources of time, effort, energy, and money—and one of that event's most prominent features might be viewed by some as spoon-feeding an interpretation of the Bible.

Both of these pastors believed that the sermons they preach change people's priorities, capacities, commitments, and behaviors, especially when people express (at the time) that they agree with the message and appreciate it. These pastors believed that their efforts to communicate were evidence of their "serious and expectant intention" to make disciples, but Willard would differ.

As a contrast to a sermon or series, Willard invites readers to imagine a church providing "a six-week seminar on how genuinely to bless someone who is spitting on you."[2] To illustrate what he expects of the seminar, Willard makes this comparison: "When you teach [that is, train] children or adults to ride a bicycle or swim, they actually do ride bikes or swim on appropriate occasions. You don't just teach them that they *ought* to ride bicycles, or that it is *good* to ride bicycles, or that they should be ashamed if they don't. Similarly, when you teach [properly train] people to bless those who curse them, they actually [will] bless those who curse them—even family members!"[3]

In Willard's opinion, the fact that such seminars do not commonly exist in churches "demonstrates beyond a doubt the lack of intention."[4] Would we ever try to teach a group of people to ride a bike or swim by giving a persuasive talk with a few tips for how to get started? Not if we wanted most of them actually to ride or swim as a habit of life from then on. Instead, if we were serious, we would put them on a bike and model how to balance; we would get into the pool with them and support them as they learn to float. So why do we try to teach people to follow Jesus in a way that we can reasonably expect *not* to work for most of the people in our church? In Willard's view, the way we conduct teaching ministry in most churches patently reveals that the church just isn't serious about bringing people into the life Jesus intends for them as a disciple.[5]

His critique may seem harsh, and even Willard describes how the ordinary state of affairs in churches really isn't any one person's fault; it's the result of a long-developing process over many years.

---

2. Willard, *The Divine Conspiracy*, 313.
3. Willard, *The Divine Conspiracy*, 314.
4. Willard, *The Divine Conspiracy*, 315.
5. Willard, *The Divine Conspiracy*, chap. 9.

But it does raise the challenge that much of what we spend our time doing in churches, even though they are good things, cannot reasonably be expected to deepen people's likeness to Christ.

Preaching is one example; pastors tend to both overestimate and underestimate its power. Without a doubt, when we preach, God does touch individual hearts and spark new beliefs, commitments, and behaviors. Nevertheless, preachers can often overestimate the impact of one sermon and underestimate the impact of ten years of sermons. It isn't realistic to expect a big impact from something that's merely stated, even if it's stated well. But it is quite realistic to expect impact from something that's *repeated and practiced*, especially when it's repeated and practiced by multiple influences in multiple settings over a long time.

The pastor whose story I told at the outset of this chapter knew this. He understood that what was far more powerful than the message he had preached that morning was the message that was delivered through multiple channels over years, reinforced by practical habits, procedures, policies, and decisions that demonstrated that the message mattered.

This is what I call a system. It is *patterned action*. We all build systems in our individual lives (even if that's not what we call them), but a system is far more powerful when it encompasses a church's life together, especially when leaders design it with intentionality.

Unfortunately, most church leaders don't spend much time doing this. They tend to invest their time in preaching individual sermons or series, managing events and ministries, and caring for those who happen to come their way. This is only natural, since those are the things they were trained to do, which have usually been modeled for them.

But observe how that time investment parallels the inadequate approaches to measuring ministry success that we looked at in previous chapters. Emphasizing preaching naturally leads us to emphasize the event where preaching takes place, and that leads us to emphasize whatever quantitative readings we can squeeze out of that event—namely, attendance and giving. Similarly, when we focus on caring for individuals only, we tend to take the pulse of the church from what those few people are telling us about their individual experiences.

Already we have seen how evaluating our efforts by general numbers and spotlighted stories makes us think we know more than we really do and obscures where most people really are in their walk with Christ. We've also seen that we have to evaluate differently, deeply, and broadly to have the information we need to truly help people. So what do we do with that information once we have it? Preaching a sermon about what we found or having the knowledge in our back pocket when we talk to an individual are good but aren't nearly enough. To make a difference in the lives of the whole community of people we're called to shepherd, we need to improve the system of patterned actions that touches the whole community. We must close the connectivity gaps that exist between our ministries and between those ministries and the outcomes God wants for people's lives.

I've talked with many leaders about designing relational systems over the years, and I generally get one of two opposite responses. One response is skepticism from leaders who doubt the value and usefulness of a system. Sometimes ministry leaders call the very notion of systems-conscious leadership flat-out unbiblical. I don't blame them for this initial reaction, because they have a point, and because I know that many of them have been burned before by system-sellers who overpromised and underdelivered.

The other response I get is from people who can't wait to learn about a new system to install in their church. But they quickly find that what I mean by "system" is radically different from what they initially expected.

Systems That Make Ministry Too Easy

In general, leaders who are in love with what they think are systems and who are eager to learn a new one are trying to fill in the blanks of a sentence like this: "If we do x, then we'll get y, which will mean z."

Decades ago, whenever I walked into the church I grew up in on a Sunday morning, I was handed a bulletin. On the back page I could find the ABCs—attendance, baptisms, and cash. The stats there told members of the congregation how many people attended the previous weekend (at worship and at Sunday school), how many baptisms had taken place over the year so far, and how much money was given.

We all were aware of those numbers because someone considered them important enough to print. We got the message that the church won by making the numbers go up. Our church had certain tried-and-true methods to do this back then, so leaders might have filled in the blanks this way:

> If we go door to door through our community on Monday nights, then we'll get more worship attenders, which will mean we're reaching our community.

If we publicize our Sunday school in the fall to families with children, then we'll get more Sunday school attenders, which will mean our church has serious disciples.

If we invite people to come forward to accept Christ and to join the church at every service, then we'll get more baptisms, which will mean we excel at evangelism.

If we do a month-long promotional campaign before we take the big special offering, then we'll get a large donation total, which will mean we're committed to missions.

Hindsight is 20/20, so let me draw some conclusions about what my childhood church believed:

The church inferred a lot from stats. We assumed that a high count of this or that was proof that our church was effective and committed, but in truth we didn't really know that.

The results the church cared most about had more to do with assimilation than with individuals' clear growth in Christ. Even if more people did attend worship or Sunday school or get baptized, we didn't know why; we merely assumed that it came from a spiritual change even though people may have had any number of other motives.

The church relied on tactics of hopeful persuasion that delivered consistent results rather than relying on a biblical pattern of disciple multiplication— or on the gospel, even though it was consistently present in our proclamation.

The church was comfortable that if someone made it through the baptism step, they would grow in their faith because of the programs offered to believers. This was assumed even though we didn't regularly examine the degree to which newly baptized people continued to engage in those programs over time and whether they actually grew if they did.

The church was pleased when people's contributions grew without necessarily knowing anything about the motives that led to that increase (for example, to elevate their influence).

I doubt leaders of the church used the word *system* much when I was a kid. But if they did, they would have considered a system to be the "if we do this" part of each sentence. They hoped and believed that if they kept working the same system from the same playbook at the time, they would keep getting the same seemingly positive results they had before.

Theological nuances or ministry approaches might look different, but to this day many people are still greatly influenced by this kind of faulty thinking. Certain if-this-then-that formulas are so engrained that some people can't imagine anything else. Formulas like these can give rise to sweeping accusations like "because you want to sunset the camp ministry, you must hate kids," or "because you want to replace the Wednesday night adult study, you don't care about the Bible" or, at the other extreme, "because you want to bring structure to engaging more people, you're not letting God do whatever he wants." Such accusations are senseless but still have their own weird logic within the world of people's deeply grooved assumptions.

In the meantime, the world, context, and people have changed, and prior approaches are not as effective as they used to be. As Nieuwhof reminds us, "The greatest enemy of your future success is always your current success."[6] Adaptable leaders recognize this and innovate new, purportedly simpler systems to replace the old ones—or at least they imitate pioneers who do. Yet, this can bring its own complications. As Bolsinger notes, "The default behavior of most organizational leaders is to solve problems *for* our organizations rather than *change our organizations* for meeting the needs of the world."[7]

Ironically, similar to the older systems I grew up with, a number of newer systems still focus primarily on assimilation—taking people from never having heard of the church to being a committed, volunteering, and giving participant. There's a thriving industry of experts who promise the right combination of tactics to maximize first-time visits, return visits, volunteer service, and so on. The way some ministry practitioners talk—and presumably

---

6. Carey Nieuwhof, *Didn't See It Coming: Overcoming the Seven Greatest Challenges That No One Expects and Everyone Experiences* (New York: WaterBrook, 2018), 104.

7. Tod Bolsinger, *Tempered Resilience: How Leaders Are Formed in the Crucible of Change* (Downers Grove, IL: InterVarsity Press, 2020), 19.

how they lead—defines a church as an assimilation system, pure and simple, and assimilation as disciple-making, period.

But the hippest, sleekest, most organic sounding system is still, at its core, based on the very same beliefs of the church of my childhood. Whether a church is clinging to a system that stopped working a generation ago or is avidly running the latest and greatest engine, the leaders who drive them are making the same mistake as the leaders before them: what they're doing is too *easy*.

I don't mean that operating the programs and protocols of a church doesn't require long hours of dogged perseverance—it certainly does. I mean that this flawed paradigm doesn't require the effort to discover where people truly are spiritually, to experiment with what genuinely helps take them deeper in their walk with Christ, to learn from the experiment, to tinker, and to try again. It doesn't require depth of creativity, ideation, or thought based on actual data. It only requires copying the same latest "innovative" thing someone else is doing, doing a different version of the same thing as before, or at most doing some new thing whose value is measured in a different *form* of participation, not widespread life change.

No matter how much planning, recruiting, rebranding, and training is necessary to construct a new assimilation system, in the end that approach is really just a quick fix. It's an attempt to move people where we want them to go without handling the messy real-life spiritual journeys of each person. Regardless of which system they choose, it presumes that leaders can keep pulling the same lever and crank out the same result—a batch of assimilated church members.

And that is precisely why leaders who are skeptical of systems reject the whole concept.

Relying on God Instead of a System

Many leaders who tune out the siren song of the next new system rightly identify the biggest problem with it: by itself, it is godless. Despite the pious language that might surround it, the system credits humans' technical competence with the power to change lives.

According to this critique of systems, Westerners have an implicit belief that if you create a finely tuned system and put people into one end of it, you will get the same results on the other end. But that is not what the Bible teaches. Only God can change the human heart; only the Holy Spirit transforms the body of Christ to live according to its true identity.

Furthermore, because God is sovereign, he does not operate on our timetable nor does he treat everyone the same. He takes each person on a unique spiritual journey according to his schedule. He's God; we can't give him orders and expect him to follow them as if he's our butler in heaven.

Therefore, as the argument goes, devising a system of spiritual progress could theoretically rob people of the freedom promised in Christ by the Holy Spirit. It could theoretically reduce people to religious machines, and rob God of his prerogative to guide people by the Word and the Spirit however he wills. One might even say that it puts God in a box.

Now, if you recall chapter 2 on reasons church leaders avoid evaluating ministry, you might have an idea of where this flawed train of thought leads, which lofts the unpredictability of God over the predictability of God. The basis of the critique contains some truth, but misapplying it to ministry can be totally mistaken.

On the one hand, without a doubt, reliance on a system of human ingenuity, even if well-meaning and subconscious, is a denial of God. It is idolatry. It functionally rejects the gospel as *the* power of God for salvation (Rom. 1:16). As Henry Blackaby puts it, "IT never works. HE works!"[8]

On the other hand, if that conviction becomes an excuse for passivity, for waiting and seeing, for preaching and praying and doing nothing more, it denies God in a different way by denying how he generally works and made people to work.

For certain, with God all things are possible. Without question, God is free to do whatever he wishes in people's lives. But if we are truly concerned about God being free to move and people being free to respond, we have to be more thoughtful about what freedom actually looks like much of the time.

For most people most often, the freedom of a blank canvas in an empty room—absolute lack of constraint or guidance—isn't freeing at all. The invitation to paint in those circumstances stymies creativity instead of unleashing it. A person doesn't know what the finished product ought to look like and doesn't know where to start, so nothing goes on the canvas. The freedom of infinite possibilities paralyzes them so that none of the potential becomes actual.

If the person does paint anything, they draw on their memory of what they've already seen, or if there's someone else painting beside them, each will be drawn to copy the other. In any case, they

---

8. Henry Blackaby and Claude V. King, *Experiencing God: Knowing and Doing the Will of God* workbook (Nashville: Lifeway, 2022), 173.

have to find some groove, some model, before they paint the first stroke. (Certainly, there are advanced artists who don't have these problems when they paint, but even they are likely to encounter the same obstacle if they are without guidance in some other area of their lives—completing a tax return, for instance.)

By contrast, if you give someone a bowl of fruit, a canvas with the spare lines of a pencil sketch on it, and a palette of colors, people paint more swiftly. Interestingly, those constraints don't make people less creative but *more*. Anyone who has visited a middle school art show has seen a row of iterations of the same basic picture, yet each one is completely unique according to the choices of the student who made it.

The same principle is at work in the spiritual life. If we say that we and the people in our churches just need to rely on the Word and the Spirit, there is an illusion of freedom. But in truth, few people exercise the freedom to take a single step unless there is a pathway for them to step on. We want to free people up to follow the Spirit to be who God made them to be, but we actually hold them back from that freedom if we don't design flexible systems along which people can grow. A person isn't really free to mature if they don't have a clear way to get started with points of reference along the way.

There's little need to dwell on this point, because all leaders already know this. As I said earlier, systems are patterned action; they are a normative way of living. And every church and minister of the gospel already has patterned actions and normative ways of living. You and your church have certain things you do every day, every week, every month, and every year. You have a calendar and a liturgy, from which you usually don't deviate (even if you might expect something unexpected to happen at certain expected times). You have a certain familiar way of talking—well-worn phrases, proverbs, principles, and mottos. You have certain predictable responses to someone's inquiry, comment, challenge, or celebration.

In other words, no matter how skeptical you are of systems, you already have one. You may not call it a system or have ever thought about it that way before, but it's there. No person can live or work without one. So the contest between system and no-system is fictitious—a false binary. *The real questions are about what system your church has, what you expect of it, and how much thoughtful intention you devote to designing it.*

It is not helpful, accurate, or intelligent to claim, "We don't rely on a system—we rely on God." Doing whatever you do regularly and asking God to bring the growth *is* your system. The fact that you operate by it implies reliance upon it. Your system may, in fact, please God, but God did not appoint any leader to lead without thinking deeply about it. Leading fatalistically abdicates responsibility to God that he bestowed on us to engage in. That is its own kind of quick fix. Beware: the enemy loves it when we shirk our responsibility in the name of Jesus.

Our Concept of System Is the Problem

So where does this leave us? If leaders who love systems and leaders who reject them are both mistaken, how are we supposed to lead?

We can start by acknowledging that critics of system-based leadership make a good point: modern people, church leaders included, are steeped in modern assumptions about systems. People think of a system as a set of consistent rules and procedures that churn out consistent results. Some leaders love that idea while others hate it. But all share a similar mental picture of what a system is.

But what if the mental picture itself is the source of the trouble? What if the big problem with leading a church by systems is a fatal misunderstanding of systems?

Today, church leaders' unconscious concept of system is heavily influenced by modern industry. We can readily picture the assembly line, the well-oiled machine, the organizational chart, and legions of workers punching in and out of a three-shift schedule, twenty-four hours a day. We can see a well-engineered arrangement of people and machines that runs like a clock and by a clock. Once the system is designed, it almost runs itself. If something breaks down, of course, it has to be fixed. And new efficiencies can always be found—how to produce the same output with less chemicals, less energy, fewer people, and thus lower costs. But the overall system is designed to be predictable.

Even though fewer of us may have personally worked in a factory compared to previous generations, we maintain a similar industrial attitude toward our surroundings. For example, we know our cars are composed of systems that are supposed to be integrated reliably so that we get predictable results every time we turn the key and step on the accelerator. The same is true for our technological devices—computers, phones, TVs, watches, gaming systems, networked appliances, and things yet to be invented. We power them on, maybe answer a few questions, and expect everything to function harmoniously with every other device.

Have you ever wondered how long people have been thinking about systems like this?

As a conception shared by most people, it's only been a few generations, dating perhaps as far back as the late nineteenth century. You might look to the Industrial Revolution that began in Britain in the late eighteenth century. You could even go back to the impersonal physics developed by Isaac Newton and his contemporaries in the late seventeenth century. Maybe you can find it in a few other unusual thinkers, but this industrial, factory-based concept of system was not prevalent in the minds of the everyday people who appear in the Bible.

No one in the civilizations in and around where the Bible was written worked in an industrial factory or had even heard of one. Industrial enterprises as we know them would not emerge until seventeen hundred years after the New Testament was written. They had no concept of systems like ours. True, there were groups of people that worked with ingenuity, and there were some factory-like situations here and there—mining, for example. But the industrial model that shapes our minds didn't shape theirs.

Does that mean that work in biblical times was unsystematic? Not at all! There was nothing either haphazard or passive about labor in ancient times, not when there was such a fine line between survival and death. People of the biblical world were highly systematic in what they did; their systems simply weren't industrial ones. Their systems, rather than being built *onto* an ecosystem, were built *into* an ecosystem. They were natural, interconnected systems because God created nature to be an interconnected system. Nature has no silos and no boxes, and neither did the occupations of the ancient world.

It is crucial to understand that the Bible frequently compares the work of church leaders to common occupations of its time, all of which were seriously concerned about systems but without our industrial presuppositions. From these preindustrial occupations we can glean insights about what a church leader ought to be doing and in what manner they ought to do it.

The most important example is shepherding, from which we get our Latin-to-English term *pastor*. Old Testament scholar Timothy S. Laniak maintains that the shepherd was the predominant metaphor for leadership in the ancient Near East. It was everywhere; for example, you might recall that in pictures on Egyptian walls and coffins, Pharaohs are often portrayed holding a shepherd's crook as a symbol of their authority to rule.[9] Every time ancient Israelites heard the story of how Moses fled to Midian to become a shepherd for forty years or how Samuel waited for Jesse to summon David from tending sheep, they said to themselves, "Of course!" The prophets often referred to kings as shepherds (as in a powerful parable in Ezekiel 34). Naturally, Jesus called himself the good shepherd (John 10:11). It was no accident that he ordered Peter to feed his lambs (John 21:15) and that Peter used the same analogy to exhort elders of the church (1 Pet. 5:1–4).

Since even fewer of us have been shepherds than have worked in a factory, the analogy is difficult for many to truly grasp today, despite our frequent use of the term in church circles. People in the ancient Mediterranean world, however, understood it well. They knew that a shepherd's knowledge and skill had to be wide-ranging

---

9. Timothy S. Laniak, *Shepherds after My Own Heart: Pastoral Traditions and Leadership in the Bible* (Downers Grove, IL: InterVarsity Press, 2006), 58–74.

and his judgment sound to an extraordinary degree. A shepherd had to know where to go in different seasons to reach water sources on time without the flock perishing on the way. He had to know when to drive them, when to give them rest, and especially when to go easy on young lambs and pregnant ewes. He had to think ahead of each stop to prevent overgrazing and starvation. He needed to know his sheep, their personalities, and their condition individually. He needed to breed them wisely, slaughter them judiciously, shear them nimbly, and mix them with goats adroitly to compose a symbiotic flock. He had to recognize signs of disease the moment they appeared. He had to be able to build and repair a pen. He had to make curds, yogurt, and cheese. He had to survive in the wilderness and prevail in death matches against wolves, lions, bears, and thieves. He had to predict weather patterns and set broken bones. And if he owned the flock, he had to hire, fire, and manage his other shepherds and train his children in everything he knew. He had to grasp local and even international economic conditions in order to buy cheap and sell dear at the right moments, and he had to negotiate with farmers to use their cleared fields as grazing land in exchange for manure from his flock.[10]

This is what church leadership is supposed to be like.

Shepherding, however, isn't the only analogy for church leadership. Another comparison is with the common profession of farming. Jesus compared himself and all who proclaim God's message with farmers planting seed (Matt. 13:3–23). Paul compared himself and Apollos to hired or tenant farmers working God's field, the church at Corinth (1 Cor. 3:5–9).

---

10. Laniak, *Shepherds after My Own Heart*, 53–57.

Like shepherds, farmers must be highly capable, vastly knowledgeable, and intensely attentive. They need to know how to care for different crops, when to fertilize, plant, and harvest, how to ward off blight and pests, how to process and store produce, how much of the yield to reserve for the next year's planting, how to breed new and better varieties of different plants, how to rotate crops for soil enrichment and conservation, how to predict and respond to changing weather, how to manage people, and how to handle variable economic conditions.

Paul also compared church leaders to builders, asserting that every leader should "be careful how he builds" because "each one's work will become obvious" (1 Cor. 3:10–15). It should go without saying that builders, architects, and civil engineers (which in those days were essentially the same thing) don't operate unsystematically. But to drive the point home, observe that the Romans of Paul's day spectacularly advanced the development of the arch, the dome, the paved road, indoor plumbing (not to mention their impressive aqueducts and sewers), radiant floor heating, and concrete.[11] Their building prowess is evident in constructions that not only still stand but still awe viewers and influence architects today.

When you start wrapping your mind around what was required of ancient shepherding, farming, building, or other occupations (fishing, for example—Mark 1:17), does any of it sound like something anyone could do well without a well-established system? Of course not!

---

11. Gallagher Flinn, "10 Cool Engineering Tricks the Romans Taught Us," How Stuff Works, February 28, 2011, https://science.howstuffworks.com /engineering/structural/10-roman-engineering-tricks.htm.

These occupations all differ from each other, yet they have certain features in common:

1. *They involve patterned activity.* There are certain functions and practices that are performed over and over again.

2. *They require keen observation of everything.* Extraordinary attention to detail is required. Refusing to read the clouds, taste the soil, smell the wind, recognize the blemish, or measure the gradient of the land even once invites failure or even disaster.

3. *They require adaptation to circumstances.* The world is both predictable in its biological, chemical, and physical laws and unpredictable in what will happen when. Workers must be continuously responsive to changing conditions to execute an approach that yields the best chance of success.

4. *They hand down a body of practical knowledge.* No one learns these trades on their own. Instead, one is initiated into an accumulation of thousands of years of empirical wisdom born of innumerable experiments over generations, and it takes a lifetime to master it.

5. *They embody a system, not systems.* Unlike mechanistic constructions that involve the interplay of multiple systems, *everything workers do is the system.* All that they do works together to form an *inter*dependent,

synergistic whole that is greater than the sum of its parts.

The Bible teaches that church leadership is supposed to be like this. It isn't building a factory that runs by itself. It also isn't speaking the right ideas and then lazily sitting back waiting for God to do the rest. Instead, biblical church leadership is an experimental, intensely attentive, continually improving effort focused on building, growing, and shepherding genuine disciple-making disciples.

Doing this well requires gaining deep knowledge of the people you lead and designing an ever-adapting, finely nuanced, integrated system that helps them grow in Christ so they're equipped to reach others in the face of constantly changing conditions. It's built for a VUCA world (volatile, uncertain, complex, ambiguous) where stubborn certainty on approaches can leave us stuck, in contrast to a flow of informed clarity that gives us nimble ways to respond flexibly as we go.[12] It's not for the lazy. There are no quick fixes. As the quote attributed to Augustine says: "Pray as though everything depends on God. Work as though everything depended on you."[13] If you don't bring to your calling the rigorous, multidirectional investigation and adaptation of a shepherd on the edge of the desert, a farmer on the edge of planting season, or a builder on the edge of a river two thousand

> We must bring to our calling rigorous biblical investigation and adaptation.

---

12. Bob Johansen, *Full-Spectrum Thinking: How to Escape Boxes in a Post-Categorical Future* (Oakland, CA: Berrett-Koehler, 2020), 34.

13. https://www.brainyquote.com/quotes/saint_augustine_165165

years ago, you're missing something. We'll explore more angles on this kind of systemic thinking in chapter 7.

Breakthrough Means Always Improving

The methodology of my PhD dissertation research was an approach called *naturalistic inquiry*. A key element of this paradigm in the world of evaluative research is the idea that in social settings, researchers must avoid manipulating outcomes due to researcher bias by establishing trustworthiness in the way they capture people's perceptions contextually. The way you get as close to understanding as possible is by collecting all the data—digging deeply to determine everyone's perspectives and realities—and looking at the same thing through multiple people's eyes.[14]

That kind of 360-degree perspective provides a basis for understanding the realities people are facing and what improvement might be appropriate in that human system. In my study of strategic process improvement, an emphasis in my doctoral work, I was struck by how what works best to improve processes in human relations management coheres with how God made things to work and how he wants leaders to lead according to the Bible. Specifically, a ministry

> You can only close connectivity gaps after you've closed awareness gaps.

---

14. This research methodology, later known as "constructivist inquiry," was largely posited in the modern era by prominent scholars Egon Guba and Yvonna Lincoln. See Yvonna S. Lincoln and Egon G. Guba, *Naturalistic Inquiry* (Newbury Park, CA: SAGE Publications, 1985).

system that produces breakthrough in many people's lives is built on breakthrough evaluation. To put it another way, you can only close the connectivity gaps between church initiatives and journey outcomes when you've closed the awareness gap. If you know where people are spiritually and the difference your church is (or isn't) making for people, you can respond and experiment to make things better. The goal is to become nimble and adaptive in changing conditions—to be intentionally responsive to where people are in their journeys—*that's* responsive leadership.

A system is never finished or perfect. A breakthrough system never reaches final form because the ever-changing world won't let it, and the people we want to help are always moving targets. Therefore, breakthrough leaders have in common a laboratory spirit of curiosity and experimentation. A leader measures what they're doing, discovers something curious, investigates, collaborates, innovates, tries something new, measures again to see what difference it made, and learns from the experience. In that sense, a good church leader is called to be an *intrapreneur,* building an innovative culture committed to *internal* improvement that impacts the whole organization.

Amid the every-which-way stresses and busyness of ministry, you might have hoped I would teach you how to make things easier. Unfortunately, it doesn't work that way; ministry takes blood, toil, tears, and sweat. What I can offer you, though, is an exhilarating way to do the same amount of work and get a lot more out of it with the results you want. It's like swinging the bat or club just as much, but the ball goes a lot further each time and gives you many more opportunities for success.

As I've claimed, there is no quick fix for the disconnects between what churches are currently doing, people's spiritual journeys, and God's desired outcomes for their lives. But there is a fix. So before we examine how to set up trains (constants) and stations (waypoints) so that they lead people to destinations (outcomes), it's important that we deconstruct other quick fixes that often distract leaders on the way. As we've seen, the debate between system and no-system is misleading. There's a similar false choice between being effective by running a lot of activities and being effective by running a few—in other words, between operating a complex ministry or a seemingly simple one. That's where we're going next.

{ CHAPTER 5 }

Why Your Simple Church Is Complicated and Your Complex Church Is Simplistic

R elax." So began the first chapter of the 2006 ministry blockbuster, *Simple Church*, by Thom Rainer and Eric Geiger. It might be the best opener of a Christian book since "In the beginning."

Rainer and Geiger knew their audience well: "Many of the church leaders we talk to are seeking an escape from the not-so-simple life." The authors wrote their book to emphasize a strong correlation between simplicity and growth in the many churches they researched, and to delineate four principles to devise a simple, focused process for making disciples. Their purpose was to show leaders a better way to arrange their church's programs than being driven by a ministry calendar that reads like a smorgasbord.[1]

---

1. Thom S. Rainer and Eric Geiger, *Simple Church: Returning to God's Process for Making Disciples* (Nashville: B&H Publishing Group, 2006), 3–4.

Nevertheless, despite the significant influence of *Simple Church*, many leaders still feel as unrelaxed as ever, still pulled in a hundred directions. In a divided, ever-changing culture, this reality has only intensified, as has the desire for increased effectiveness in the midst of change. Even if leaders can rattle off their disciple-making strategy in crisp words like "gather, grow, go" or "believe, belong, become," they still encounter one complication after another as they seek to shepherd and mobilize their people week to week.

Why? Because many leaders have not grasped the complexity of simplicity. Misunderstanding, misappropriating, or misapplying the tenets of simplicity makes for skin-deep simplicity—I call it being a "seemingly simple" church. A church that emblazons three bold words or phrases in its communication or strips down the calendar might *seem* simple at first, but is it *actually* simple? Your perspective has to be much more sophisticated if you want to focus your attention in a way that improves your *effectiveness*. As my colleague Bryan Rose once said: "It is a simple thing to maintain complexity, but it is a complex thing to maintain simplicity."[2]

The trouble is that many leaders, harried by responsibilities, incorrectly took from the simplicity conversation that running many programs is inherently complicated and running few programs is inherently simple. If that were true, then slashing things from the calendar, retooling programs to make them more or less alike, or even merely pasting the same label over a conglomeration of ministries that don't actually have much to do with each other

---

2. Bryan Rose, "23 Things You're Still Doing . . . Even Though You Read 'Simple Church,'" Launch Clarity, February 8, 2019, https://launchclarity com/2019/02/08/23-things-youre-still-doing-even-though-you-read-simple -church.

should result in a more effective, focused ministry. But that's just not what happens in many churches—ministry eventually gets as complicated as before, just with shifted challenges that emerge over time.

What makes churches complicated isn't the number of programs but rather the lack of connectivity between programs. Focused ministry isn't necessarily about having fewer programs; it's about having the right programs for your unique church that are wisely connected to each other *and result in the clearly defined outcomes you're aiming for in people's lives on their journeys.* In other words, to use the predominant metaphor of this book, the focus you're looking for comes from minding the connectivity gap by having trains that reliably connect to stations and proceed to destinations.

> What makes churches complicated isn't the number of programs but rather the lack of connectivity between programs.

Though there certainly are cases when decreasing your programs after a thorough outcomes-based evaluation is wise, focusing on fewer things doesn't automatically make you more effective and sometimes *hinders* your ability to reach the outcomes you desire for people. That happens when you've inadvertently removed or haven't implemented important contributing steps that move people to deepen the outcome expressions of their lives. It's like there are sections of washed-out train tracks (or entire lines that are missing) on people's journeys. Disconcertedly, in the name of simplicity, many leaders are the very ones who wash out their own tracks and act like the train is supposed to operate just fine in reaching its destination. As you focus more intently, you might actually need to *add* constants or waypoints in certain areas based on the outcome growth (or lack thereof) you learn about in your people's lives.

Being simple or focused does not and should not mean "what's easy for leaders." It means "what's effective for followers." Simple should never be simplistic. The focus should be on what connectivity is *needed* based on where your people are on their journeys in relation to the outcome expressions you've defined. In other words, an effective disciple-making system requires a carefully designed pathway informed by evaluation that brings unity to people's diverse spiritual journeys without ignoring their individuality. It's easy to say "amen" to this; it's even easy to think that you're doing it. It's a lot harder to *actually* do it.

Leading a church that continually increases its effectiveness by minding the gap requires a deeper understanding of focus, constant attention to what's really happening in people's lives throughout the body, and a research lab ethos on your leadership team. Without these qualities, pastors will often unintentionally lead in a simplistic way that hinders their effectiveness. And remember, simple should never be simplistic.

Errors of simplistic thinking apply across a spectrum. The errors relate to overly simplistic mindsets that many pastors default to if they're not careful. It's important to know what your tendency might be so you can avoid it. On one end of the simplistic thinking spectrum, pastors lead toward a seemingly simple church with fewer programs that ends up being too limited and complicated to shepherd widespread growth in,

> Simple should never be simplistic.

given the realities of people's lives. On the other end of the spectrum, pastors lead toward a complex church demonstrating simplistic thinking that offering more will somehow lead to more growth. Many churches, perhaps yours, land somewhere in between, though most have a tendency to lean one way or the other.

ERRORS OF SIMPLISTIC THINKING
Mindsets that Hinder Effectiveness

Simplistically Complex	Seemingly Simple
We err by thinking **more** programs will lead to progress	We err by thinking **fewer** programs will lead to progress

Regardless of your tendency, the *number* of programs you choose to have does not automatically lead to greater effectiveness. Your goal should be to get off the spectrum in your thinking. Instead, focus on evaluating the trains and stations your people actually need based on their progress toward the destinations you're seeking. That may mean you need fewer, more, or the same number of programs compared to what you have now. The power of simplicity does not come from the number; it comes from having a way to clearly evaluate and improve your connectivity.

In this chapter we'll explore the ironies of simplistic thinking so you can discover where your church might fall. First, let's start by discussing the complex church.

The Simplistic Mindset That Befalls Complex Churches

When I talk about a complex church, I mean a church with a myriad of ministry activities whose leaders or staff may sometimes feel like they're functioning more like event managers or platform performers than trainers of disciple makers.

Churches have been complex for generations. In many communities years ago, churches were hubs for activity; if it wasn't happening in or around the church, it probably wasn't happening. Even small churches were bursting with committees that devoted countless hours to a wide array of activities. This approach rose to a new scale in the 1980s and 1990s when mushrooming megachurches leveraged their resources to pile something-for-everyone ministries into gigantic menus of options. It's not surprising that master consultant Lyle Schaller published a book entitled *The Seven-Day-a-Week Church*.[3] Even after the global pandemic that emerged in 2020, many churches sought ways to start or re-start *more* initiatives to help things feel like more was being accomplished again.

In a church like this, when you look at things like the ministry calendar, web site map, or organizational chart, things look really complex. But I propose that this sort of church, no matter how complex it seems, is actually far too simplistic in its thinking.

---

3. Lyle E. Schaller, *The Seven-Day-a-Week Church* (Nashville: Abingdon Press, 1992).

Ironically, complex churches succumb to a *simplistic philosophy of ministry* that dramatically hinders their effectiveness. I'm not talking about how pastors in the church would answer if asked directly, "What's your philosophy of ministry?" They may have given that quite a bit of thought over the years and likely have much nuanced wisdom to offer. Rather, I'm addressing the philosophy implied by the choices leaders make and the initiatives they manage year in and year out.

The flawed, simplistic ministry philosophy that lives in complex churches is, in a nutshell, that more activity yields more life-change. It is the erroneous idea that the more we do as a church—more importantly, the more that people do in our church—the more people grow in Christ.[4] I don't believe that leaders consciously believe this—quite the contrary. But they may hold this assumption without even realizing it. It reveals itself in how complex churches operate and how they make decisions, and significant consequences flow from it.

For one, this simplistic philosophy of ministry generates overly *simplistic solutions to problems*. For example, when I met the leaders of a long-established city church, it boasted three hundred deacons. You read that right. If there were ever a church that believed if one is good, more is better, it was this church. Yet its small army of deacons was also a testament to the exceptional initiative and leadership talent among its laypeople. Consequently, whenever a new need was identified—a problem in people's lives, a tightly defined

---

4. This is supported by the research findings of Rainer and Geiger in *Simple Church*, 3–4. See also Willow Creek's Reveal study in Greg L. Hawkins and Cally Parkinson, *Move: What 1,000 Churches Reveal about Spiritual Growth* (Grand Rapids: Zondervan, 2011), 16–18.

demographic cohort not being reached, and so on—with the best of intentions, the church's impulse was to add a ministry to the menu. If someone said to the staff, "Let's do this," it was often done. The new initiative typically entailed a name, a committee, a spot on the calendar, a space in the building, a line in the bulletin, possibly even a new staff member (or at least a new item on the job description of a current staff member). Even as the church's suite of activities got mind-boggling complex, it all was driven by a simplistic mindset to addressing needs. Just add more, even if adding more siphoned energy and unintentionally caused the church's impact to become more shallow by the day.

Some complicated churches may use other simplistic problem-solving methods such as "we do whatever worked well in the past" or "we do whatever brings people in." One church with twenty-seven committees (again, you read that right) responded to steady decline with the plea, "What can we provide for young families to do?" to which a colleague of mine responded, "What young family is looking for *more* to do?" It's just another example of a flawed, simplistic solution arising from the simplistic ministry philosophy of "more."

The philosophy of more also imprints an overly *simplistic concept of discipleship* on people. People in our churches don't always believe what we tell them, but if they spend enough time with us, they often come to believe what we model for them. We can preach till we're blue in the face that growth in the Christian life comes by growing in grace, faith, and the Holy Spirit. But in a complex church, the unspoken, much more powerful message is "do more activities, grow more spiritually." If one Bible study or serving role is good, two or three must be better, right? Yet there is typically little care taken to find out if any of the Bible studies or any of the roles produce real, lasting fruit in a person's life other than a longer checklist of what they've participated in.

A person formed in an environment like this understandably but erroneously concludes that more activity really does yield more life-change. So, if they want to experience a life changed by Christ, they need to be doing more stuff. In some people, this promotes guilt. In others, it promotes self-righteousness or at least contentedness: "If I go to church as often as I can, go to a group as often as I can, give a little more money, and read a little more Bible, I'm a good Christian, or at least better than most others out there. And if I don't, I'm not."

One heart-breaking example of this is from a community group of married couples at a large church who had been together for years, studying the Word and assuming that they were caring for one another. But ultimately, half of their couples divorced. The couples who were struggling signed up for more and more service opportunities in the church, believing that greater church activity should help their marriage. When it all came crashing down, other members of the group were shocked that they had no idea what really was happening.

An alternative but just as dangerous message is "do what you like—pick from anything we offer (like ordering your favorite item on a lunch menu)—and you'll grow spiritually." The something-for-everyone approach communicates that the attender's preference is the most important factor and that growth in Christ revolves around just doing what you prefer. In any case, whether by doing what they like or doing more, people are discipled into a flawed, simplistic notion of what discipleship is. This is because, in the absence of clear pathways to understand and grow in defined out-comes, their decision-making isn't well informed by what they most *need*.

Finally, a simplistic philosophy of ministry results in an overly *simplistic evaluation of effectiveness* when we reflect on what we're doing. Sometimes our self-evaluation is based on quantity, the idea that we must be doing a good job because we're doing so much or because people are attending. Sometimes it's based on quality by spotlighting individuals whose lives *are* being changed as if they represent the whole (which they don't), as was discussed in an ear-lier chapter.

Simplistic ministry philosophy and simplistic ministry evalua-tion reinforce each other. If we believe that doing more does more, we think a quick glance at our activity participation tells us our impact. Conversely, if we measure activity broadly but only mea-sure transformation narrowly, it gives us the false assumption that what we're doing is working. As long as we keep going this way, we're never compelled by true measurement to find out whether we're merely a glorified, faith-based community center or a truly mobilized, well-trained army of people throughout the church who are personally and deeply engaged in multiplying disciple makers. We remain shackled to a well-intentioned but simplistic paradigm.

The Seemingly Simple Church
That Feels Complicated

When I talk about a seemingly simple church—the opposite of the complex church—I'm talking about a church that seeks to be simple in the way it organizes ministry but errs by thinking simplistically instead. This church probably has a set of two to five steps or programs that are intended to lead someone from being a newcomer to being an integrated participant in the church. This church may even pride itself on these few programs being the main or only ones they do. In fact, "program" itself might be a dirty word among some of their leaders.

Seemingly simple churches often use short, catchy words or phrases to describe each part of their process, which in and of itself can be a helpful communication tool. But what it boils down to for most of them is the familiar combination of worship services, groups, and volunteer service, regardless of the creative language that might be applied to them. (Sometimes a separate deeper Bible study track or new members' class is included, perhaps with a here's-your-spiritual-gift-and-place-you-can-serve diagnostic workup.)

On the surface, the worship-groups-service triad is a powerful starting point, and does seem quite simple in a good way— far simpler than the complicated, something-for-everyone church. The great majority of church leaders over the past few decades have longed to get this simple. Yet *seemingly* simple churches are often a good deal more complicated than they appear at first, because they are much more simplistic than actually simple.

Seemingly simple churches believe that focus means just doing a few things. But by itself, that isn't focus—it's actually empty. Ironically, that false simplicity makes leaders' lives more complicated given the realities of ministering to people's complex needs as you seek to shepherd them on their journeys.

My friend Cory Hartman told me a story that beautifully illustrates what I'm talking about. Years ago, his dad, Daryl, was driving his 1990 Pontiac Grand Am when the standard transmission started giving out. His left foot could feel the clutch weakening; he knew that whatever gear he shifted into, he would not be able to shift out of it again. Home was thirty miles away. With fleeting seconds to decide, he jammed the stick awkwardly into third gear before the clutch pedal gave way completely.

Daryl figured that third gear could handle most of the range of speed he absolutely had to operate in. He could rev the engine high to travel at a moderate speed, and if he had to slow down, as long as he didn't stop, he could probably barely, ever so slowly get the car to rumble and shake up to speed again.

In one respect, Daryl's drive got simpler; he no longer had to worry about shifting gears, because there was now only one option. That complex element of driving was entirely removed.

But as you can imagine, the seeming simplicity of driving in one gear made his trip much more complicated! He had to change his destination to the dealership where he got the car serviced. He had to figure out the best route to get there from where he was, which happened to proceed through an area he wasn't very familiar with, long before GPS directions. He had to map that route on roads that wouldn't require him to go too fast but that also contained as few traffic lights as possible. And when he got to a traffic light, he had to gauge how fast to go to get through it before it turned red or how slow to go so that the wheels were still rolling when the light turned green.

Just as simplistic driving makes for a complicated trip, simplistic strategy makes for complicated ministry. Over the last twenty or more years, perhaps the biggest manifestation of seemingly simple ministry strategy has involved small groups. As people became less inclined to give more than two or three timeslots to church activities each week, numerous ministries were ruthlessly cut away in many churches, and small groups evolved into the do-everything teaching, community, evangelism, service, and support option. In other words, small groups became the third gear of church programming.

But this seemingly simple strategy has caused complications for many leaders in many churches. A pastor of a large suburban church was asked by a respected leadership expert, "Why do you do a men's retreat every year?" The pastor couldn't immediately think of a reason. "If you don't have a reason," the expert continued, "why are you doing it?" Driven where he thought the logic led, the pastor abolished men's and women's ministries in the church and concluded that small groups would fill the gap. But there were still many men and women who had plenty of important reasons that these ministries fueled distinct discipleship and missional outcomes. Both their protests as well as the gaping holes left in the church's discipleship pathway caused significant complications! Years later, after more clearly defining their journey outcomes, the church realized the huge mistake and added comprehensive men's and women's ministries—not because of complaints—but because of the important roles they played in the disciple-making pathway *for that church's defined outcomes.*

Another large multisite church that thought they had a simple strategy made a big push to get everyone in a group—get in a group, *any* group. But the groups varied widely; they included couples' groups, men's groups, women's groups, Bible study groups, support groups, issue-focused groups, service groups, seeker groups, and on and on. The assumption was that just getting people into some kind of group was good enough. But the groups were so diverse and unlike each other with no clarity on outcomes that managing the whole thing as if it were one simple ministry became impossible. There was no true way to know whether groups were actually achieving desired disciple-making or missional outcomes beyond a few testimonies here and there. Moreover, because the groups were disconnected, there was no obvious reason why someone should attend one rather than another beyond mere instinctive preference. This naturally fostered the same sort of do-what-you-want mindset found in a complex church with program overload—or worse, no different than a community center that offers a menu of various activities.

Another manifestation of the seemingly simple groups strategy is the decline of consistent mid-sized Sunday morning studies or gatherings. To achieve a format that was perceived to foster greater transparency and accountability, many churches ended them or moved them out of the spotlight in favor of home-based small groups. Increased transparency and accountability are certainly important, but many churches learned that they inadvertently threw the baby out with the bathwater. They failed to account for the reality that a consistent ongoing adult group of fifty to eighty people can offer a different, important community dynamic compared to a home group of ten to twenty people. Specifically, while some people latch on to smaller groups in homes easily, others do not. Many learned that regular connection in mid-sized groups provides a different but significant asset in community building, mobilization around discipleship and missional outcomes, and even the practical meeting of needs that smaller groups struggle to emulate. Functioning as the body of Christ inside and outside the church can sputter when too much emphasis is placed on smaller groups. One twenty-six-year-old who was active in a large church without substantive mid-sized opportunities might have phrased this limitation best: "I'm with my home group all the time, but it feels like the church is constantly quarantining me and everyone else from the rest of the body"—a complicated problem brought about by a seemingly simple strategy.

Another example of the problem of seemingly simple strategy is support ministries for people dealing with significant challenges. For instance, recent decades have seen an increase in discipleship material for those who struggle with addictions. Addictions are complicated problems. But in order to fit into the program structure of seemingly simple churches, the tools are often structured in the form of six- or twelve-week group studies. Despite the considerable value of these studies, this is a case where form doesn't follow function. Instead, function is crammed into a preexisting form. Addictions aren't broken in six to twelve weeks; as the complications of recovery roll on, the seemingly simple structure isn't equipped to address them.

Life is complicated, people are complicated, and therefore, ministry is complicated. But when leaders with good intentions devise a seemingly simple strategy, it doesn't resolve the complications; instead, it pushes them aside or onto people less equipped to handle them. When smaller groups are made the linchpin of community, there are generally two alternative results for a group. Either the group does not exhibit enough openness toward one another for their life complications to come out (at least until a couple blindsides the group with an announcement that they are getting divorced), or group members do reveal their complicated lives, and it quickly becomes apparent that the volunteer small group leader isn't adequately trained to help. Then the pastoral staff has to react like firefighters responding to a call, and all over again they face the complications they had tried to delegate away.

In complex churches, when people aren't engaged participants, leaders typically assume that the responsibility lies with themselves to create something more compelling. But in seemingly simple churches, leaders tend to be so overconfident in the elegance of their system that they tend to blame people for not participating in it. For instance, in a church with one main relational environment—let's say midweek sermon-based small groups—staff may be annoyed at how difficult it is to get everyone to join. Yet it may never cross the leaders' minds that there are people in their church whose next move to follow Jesus isn't activated by a midweek sermon-based small group, yet changing the size or focus of the group, clarifying missional opportunities or desired outcomes, or providing options to attend before or after weekend worship could turn the key.

We err if we think of simplicity as a small number of activities. Instead, the kind of focus we should seek is the intelligent connection of activities and outcomes that accords with how the Holy Spirit is moving in different people's lives. Focus isn't three words on a web site; it is what a disciple *experiences* when she is led by thoughtful, diligent shepherds to the right next step for her as an individual based on her growth in outcomes on the journey. Any other strategic approach is at once oversimplistic and overcomplicated.

> A simple focus isn't three words on a web site.

A Better, More Agile Way

The church with a hundred things going on and the church with five things going on look quite different. The week-to-week work of their leaders feels quite different. But they often have in common a certain complacency, perhaps even a subtle laziness.

This has nothing to do with how hard they're working or how devoted they are to the work God has given them; I've met many exhausted pastors who desperately need replenishment. Rather, it has to do with *how they think* about what they're doing. It's that they think because they're working so hard and are so devoted, and because they can point either to a profusion of activities or to a minimalistic program structure, they have therefore done their duty. But that isn't actually true.

Minding the gap for deeper life transformation based on your church's outcome expressions brings ongoing revitalization because you can focus on the right things at the right times in the right ways. It involves a continual and exhilarating combination of breakthrough evaluation, connectivity, engagement of others, and responsiveness to where your people are and where you're heading together.

Consider the qualities outlined in the following self-assessment. If you're not completely familiar with all of the terms, don't worry—we'll be diving into them more in the upcoming chapters.

THE MINISTRY GAP ASSESSMENT

For each of the four statements below, rate your agreement on a scale from one to seven (1–7) using the descriptions under each one as a guide.

1. All of our ministries are clearly designed to move people toward our church's defined outcome expressions of Christlikeness in knowledge, character, and action.

> 1 = Our senior leaders are interested in more clearly defining the journey outcomes and specific expressions we're seeking to move people toward.

> 3 = Our senior leaders have defined a robust, well-rounded set of written journey outcomes and specific expressions we're seeking and know how to use them to prioritize daily decisions.

> 5 = Our senior leaders have a system in place to regularly measure a broad and representative cross-section of our church to evaluate progress toward defined outcomes (such as a Mind the Gap Survey).

> 7 = Our senior leaders can verify and validate with data how at least 85 percent of our ministries are moving people toward the journey outcomes and expressions we have defined.

> Rating (1–7): _____

2. Our ministries are all thoughtfully connected to each other as an organic whole, each playing a clearly defined part, rather

than feeling like a variety of activities that sometimes seem unrelated.

> 1 = Our senior leaders want to grasp the distinction between thoughtful connectivity and unrelated activities.

> 3 = Our senior leaders all firmly grasp what thoughtful connectivity of ministry waypoints and constants looks like and can clearly articulate how it differs from a collection of unrelated activities.

> 5 = Our senior leaders all can clearly articulate a thorough, realistic evaluation of each of our ministries and how close we are to the ideal of thoughtful connectivity between all of them.

> 7 = Our senior leaders can verify and validate that at least 85 percent of our ministries are thoughtfully connected as waypoints and constants, each playing a clearly articulated part that relates to the others in our defined system.

> Rating (1–7): _____

3. Our senior leaders are making continual progress toward our outcomes using checkup loops with on-the-ground lay partners (metapartners) throughout our church.

> 1 = Our senior leaders want to learn more about the idea of involving lay leaders more deeply as on-the-ground metapartners and how they can support us through checkup loops.

3 = Our senior leaders can clearly articulate what metapartners are, what the five steps in a consistent checkup loop are, and their importance in discipling people toward our journey outcomes.

5 = Our senior leaders have named the metapartners they're regularly connecting with in the steps of a checkup loop and have reliably estimated the percentage of the congregation these partners are in regular touch with.

7 = Our senior leaders can validate that at least 85 percent of church staff and lay leaders are actively and consistently engaged in (or facilitating) our system of metapartners and checkup loops.

Rating (1-7): _____

4. Our senior leaders have a regular rhythm of adapting and reshaping ministries based on people's progress toward defined outcomes and insight from metapartners.

1 = Our senior leaders want to understand better how clear evaluation and checkup loops would enable us to nimbly adjust and reshape ministries.

3 = Our senior leaders know how to adjust and reshape ministries continually and appropriately according to clear evaluation and checkup loop feedback.

5 = Our senior leaders have scheduled when they will consider and implement adjustments to ministries based on people's progress toward outcomes and insight from our metapartners.

7 = Our senior leaders can validate that ministries are evaluated and adjusted based on people's measured progress toward outcomes and metapartner insight at least bi-monthly (calibration rhythm of 6+ times per year).

Rating (1–7): _____

	Score
Statement 1: Evaluation	
Statement 2: Connectivity	
Statement 3: Metapartnering	
Statement 4: Responsiveness	
TOTAL	

Total Score

4–15 = Our church is overly simplistic or complicated

16–23 = Our church is on its way to minding the gap

24–28 = Our church is proactively minding the gap

At first, this initial self-assessment may leave you with more questions than answers. Although we looked at evaluation closely in previous chapters, you may be wondering, *What does it look like to have thoughtfully connected ministries? What are on-the-ground metapartners and checkup loops, and how do they help? And how do we practically adjust what we're doing according to what we find?* These questions will all be answered in the rest of this book. In the next chapter, we'll look closer at how good connectivity of constants and waypoints practically works, leading to breakthrough.

CHAPTER 6

Breakthrough: Unlocking the Power of Connectivity

On a brisk, sunny morning a few years ago, I took a trip from my home in the Dallas area to meet with a client in Des Moines, Iowa. It was a familiar journey I had made before—a simple 90-minute, nonstop flight. But this time the simple trip got very complicated.

Halfway through the flight, the pilot announced to the passengers that intense, quickly moving winter storms in the Midwest had cut off our route to Des Moines, so we would be heading to Chicago's O'Hare International Airport instead. But once we got to Chicago and circled the airport for well over an hour, that airport closed as well and we were redirected to Chicago's other airport, Midway. After maintaining a holding pattern *there* for quite some time, Midway determined that it couldn't take us either, so we were sent southwest 250 miles to St. Louis. Another hour later we touched down, but so had a hundred other diverted planes with no room for them at any gate because so many departing flights had been cancelled. All these planes, including my own, were parked on the tarmac far from the terminal with nowhere to go. For hours, thousands of passengers were stuck inside their planes.

While standing near my seat to stretch a bit, I made the situation into a game by researching how I might piece together an unlikely route that could get me to my destination . . . or at least somewhat closer to my destination. If I were going to be stranded, it didn't really matter *where*. I thought I might as well try to make it an adventure along the way.

As I explored different routes, I was surprised to find a series of three not yet canceled regional flights that could get me from St. Louis to Detroit to Minneapolis to Des Moines late that night. They were tough connections and many things would have to go just right, but it was possible in theory. The hardest part was somehow getting from the plane to the terminal a hundred yards away to begin my quest.

I chatted with a flight attendant to tell her what I found, and graciously asked if there might be any way I could get out of the plane and into the airport. I was expecting a response along the lines of, "Are you crazy?! Do you see where we are out here?" But instead, she paused and excused herself for a moment. When she returned, she spoke in a hushed voice. "You only have a carry-on, right? I just talked to the pilot; he happens to be from Iowa. Casually get your bag, and meet me at the back of the plane in two minutes."

Suddenly feeling like either a VIP or a spy in an action thriller, I stood, got my things, and strode resolutely down the aisle, ignoring a few curious stares from others. In a flash, the flight attendant swung open a hidden door in the very back of the plane, said "go," and I darted down a small set of stairs that descended to the tarmac. At the foot of the stairs were two armed security guards who quickly ushered me into a black van and sped me under the wings of the plane, down the runway, and all the way to an external nondescript stairway between two jet bridges of the airport. At the top of the metal stairs, I pulled open the door, stepped inside, and suddenly found myself in the middle of the terminal. When I looked back and saw nothing but identical, nondescript panels running along the wall, I realized I had come through a literal secret entrance!

Now inside, I put my complex plan into action and was on my way. Much later that night, seventeen and a half hours and four flights from when I started, I collapsed on the bed in my Des Moines hotel room.

That trip is one of my favorite stories to tell, and confidentially, I can't help but enjoy it as a satisfying achievement. But I'm certainly glad it's not the norm. It would be a nightmare if I had to deal with that much complication every time I traveled.

In the previous chapter, I asserted that effective focus in ministry isn't necessarily a minimalistic calendar. Rather, it is the disciple's experience of being led seamlessly to the right next step on their individual journey with Christ. It's the sort of thing I experience on my very best trips. There is detailed intentionality going on behind the scenes that I'm not aware of, but from my point of view as a traveler, my next move toward my destination seems clear and straightforward.

I experience a version of this when I go to one of my favorite places: Walt Disney World. Disney parks give their millions of fans many reasons to love them and keep returning, but the biggest reason I appreciate Disney is the extreme attention to detail that captures guests' attention and immerses them in the larger story. This is especially noticeable if you go when crowds are light, or if you take time to step back and observe. I am so fascinated by it that I have studied Disney's techniques, experienced their training, and taken days at Disney parks to do the most complete behind-the-scenes tours I can get.

Disney makes an extraordinarily complex array of detail into a sequence of natural next steps that draws a person further into an immersive experience. There are countless examples of this. The buildings on Main Street gradually decrease in height as they near Cinderella's Castle, which draw the guest's eye to the castle and make it appear larger. When you move from one area to another, every sense tells you that you've entered a new place—not only the look of it but also the fragrance in the air, the feel of different pathway textures under your feet, and the distinct sounds that draw you in (ingenious acoustic engineering making sonic barriers between one place and another). When you relax on a bench off the beaten path of Main Street, you might even hear the faint sounds of a dance lesson happening on the floor above you—all entirely simulated on a recording from discreet speakers. I could go on and on, but you get the idea.

The critical question is this: Is the experience of a participant in your church more like being part of something as intentional as that, or is it more like Clint Grider's trip from Dallas to Des Moines? Does your ministry system immerse people in an environment that naturally leads them to the next steps Christ has for them? Or do they have to contend with a disjointed system that inadvertently requires dogged determination, heroic ingenuity, and extraordinary assistance to connect the dots?

This chapter and the ones that follow are about how to make your church a place that captures peoples' attention and hearts in ways that are deeper and more far-reaching than you ever imagined. It's *not* about how to make your church "the happiest place on earth" and get people to spend a lot of money; it's about cooperating with the Holy Spirit to facilitate people's next moves for breakthrough growth in Christ for his kingdom purposes. As Andrew Hébert says in his book, *Shepherding like Jesus*, "It's all about him. It's not about me. The moment my ministry is about me [or anything else really], it's not about him."[1]

How Disney World Captivates Guests

Disney parks possess one feature that's especially illuminating in designing an immersive experience that feels beautifully simple to the person who enters it.

On one hand, Disney parks consist of meticulously cultivated environments. When you enter any of the "lands" of Magic Kingdom or other parks, you enter a *place*. They establish a rich atmosphere that heightens awareness and works on you while you're in each place.

On the other hand, the parks also punctuate the atmosphere with special happenings that capture guests' attention for a few moments at a time. These might include a parade, a beloved Disney character, or an apparent custodian who suddenly becomes a street performer by using his wet mop to draw a character on the street to the delight of a child passing by. Even the timely approach of

---

1. Andrew Hébert, *Shepherding like Jesus: Returning to the Wild Idea That Character Matters in Ministry* (Nashville: B&H Publishing Group, 2020), 90.

a cast member offering perfectly tailored assistance falls into this category.[2]

Here is a major part of the genius of Disney parks. Disney carefully combines cultivated environments and special ("magical") happenings to captivate guests. It takes both working together to create an immersive experience that moves people.

Counterexamples show us why. Imagine, for instance, that Disney World only had special happenings but no cultivated environments. A barbershop quartet, dancing marching band, or Donald Duck might be noteworthy, but no one would travel from far and wide to see them in a parking lot.

On the flip side, imagine a Disney World with rich environments but nothing happening in them. The immersive atmosphere of Frontierland might be enjoyable to see once, but if nothing interesting occurs there, no one would stay very long before heading home.

These elements at Disney parks that I'm calling environments and happenings parallel the two basic kinds of intentional activities in a church. The environments at a Disney park are like *constants*, the ongoing experiences that happen in and through the church week after week. Constants include programs like worship services, groups, classes, and regular volunteering as well as an individual's disciplines for spiritual growth like daily Bible reading and prayer. In the analogy of the Underground, constants are represented by trains; they should provide the *perpetual movement* that carries a

---

2. For more detail on how Disney creates special moments for guests, see J. Jeff Kober, *The Wonderful World of Customer Service at Disney*, 2nd ed. (Kissimmee, FL: Performance Journeys, 2020), 70–76.

person to the destinations of Christlikeness as they are ridden over time.

On the other hand, the special happenings that occur at a Disney park are like *waypoints,* the momentary, short-run, or temporary experiences that are meant to inspire someone to a new practice or a change of direction. Waypoints might include a catalytic training event, a four-week all-church group emphasis, or counseling about a particular challenge. Waypoints should be *pivotal moments.* In the analogy of the Underground, they are the stations that lead someone to ride a new train, whether an activity done in community with other church travelers or a practice in their personal life.

Churches help people experience something new and wonderful about God when environments and happenings—that is, constants and waypoints, trains and stations—are working together. That's connectivity—when your constants and waypoints are seamlessly integrated to complement one another in a system. Without both, people rarely experience breakthrough, and they usually don't travel as far with Christ toward the destinations he desires for them.

Nonstop, Hyped-Up, or Ho-Hum?

Churches experience different results depending on whether they concentrate energy on their constants, on their waypoints, on neither, or on both. A brief tour helps to explain why you're getting the results you're getting in your own church.

Let's look first at a church that focuses its effort on making its constants (trains) excellent. I call this a *nonstop church.* Its robust suite of constants provides ongoing spiritual nourishment and challenge for people in a variety of ways. Yet because there are few inspiring and well-coordinated waypoints, people rarely take decisive steps into a new engagement or behavior.

In a nonstop church, people who are used to only attending worship rarely join a smaller group and people who are used to their group rarely engage much more deeply other than through a few events here and there. People don't often make decisive changes in their personal lives, because a summons to something new doesn't feel different at a deep level; the call to action just blends in with the rest of the busy routine. It's like the classic folk song "M.T.A.," a ballad about an unfortunate man named Charlie who starts riding Boston's subway system one day but can never get off. A better way to look at it is as a train that never slows down for new riders to get on.

One historic, small-town church had quite a complicated calendar for its small size. On top of its constants—Sunday worship with children's programs, Sunday school with graded classes, midweek Bible study and children's events, choir practice, a women's missionary support group, and a weekly health program—it layered on misconnected waypoints like musical productions, guest concerts, bimonthly social events, vacation Bible school, youth lock-ins, a booth at seasonal festivals on Main Street, an annual picnic, and a camping weekend (tired yet?).

The pastor could readily see the huge volume of hours required to make all these activities go. He could also see the anxiety on the faces of the overstretched volunteers who toiled to pull them off. But he could not see much disciple-making value in most of the activities. He believed that if they instead focused on a smaller number of constants that were laid out for people as simple next steps, people would naturally take those steps, participate in constants, and grow. So, through a combination of consolidation and volunteer attrition, the church evolved into a "simple" program structure that reduced constants and virtually eliminated waypoints.

But merely having fewer programs did not generate growth. Something still wasn't working. To give the system a jolt, from time to time the church rallied to do a special event waypoint to grab attention and raise enthusiasm. Unfortunately, these produced few lasting, observable results in large part because they weren't carefully tied to evaluation of people's condition on the front end and to a constant as a next logical step on the back end. Eventually even these waypoints were given up, and the church succumbed to no growth and even decline despite (or because of) its seemingly simple, constant-exclusive programming.

While some churches like this one have trains but no connected stations, other churches put too much emphasis on stations and too little on trains. I call this a *hyped-up church*. The carefully planned waypoints of a hyped-up church produce great excitement and sometimes even a raft of decisions to follow Christ, to give sacrificially, to serve the community, or to make another major commitment. But without effective and well-coordinated constants, there is no follow-through, and people's commitments don't usually result in lasting change.

In a hyped-up church, people are wowed by a special worship or musical event, but don't worship God throughout the week. They participate in Community Cleanup Day, but don't start serving their next-door neighbor day to day. They experience tear-soaked inner healing at an occasional retreat or conference, but don't establish accountable habits with a microgroup to live out the healing when they get home. Instead of taking trains to a destination, it's as if they get shot out of a cannon from one station to another.

Some waypoints seem great in the moment, but they don't actually work—in other words, people have a great time and maybe even have a brief mountaintop encounter with God, and they give the event glowing reviews, yet there is no lasting difference in their lives. In other cases, however, the unrealistic expectations that leaders in a hyped-up church expect out of waypoints actually make them bad experiences even while they're happening.

One large church wanted to restart a men's ministry, so leaders planned a well-advertised waypoint that was intended to gather men and launch them into growth in Christ and community with one another. This was the first men's event at the church in years, so hundreds of guys signed up, curious to learn more about what the church was launching.

When they arrived at the church building, they found snacks and cornhole boards set up outside the worship center. It would have been a fun way to pass the time if attenders already knew each other, but most were strangers because there hadn't been any regular ways for men to connect in the church, and few took the initiative to start a game. Most guys stood around the space with a soft drink either awkwardly trying to introduce themselves or asking others if they knew anything about what the event was about.

After a while, the men filtered into an adjacent room for the main program. The room was packed. Chairs had been set up with no space between them at all, putting attenders in uncomfortably close proximity with one another. Then, the music started, featuring a hefty portion of songs with lyrics about being deeply in love with Jesus. The singers on the small stage seemed really into it, but sideways glances from the audience revealed that most of the men were mumbling with arms crossed just hoping to get through it as quickly as possible.

At the close of the set, a young leader got up to pray. Almost in tears, he prayed loudly how the leaders had been "longing for this night so the men could open up their lives" and for God to "break everyone's heart tonight." This was followed by testimonies of men who had experienced God's power in their lives. One man had been addicted to hard drugs. Another man had lost a daughter. They were wonderful witnesses to God's amazing grace, yet they were also highly intense, emotionally exhausting stories.

After the large group time, it was announced that everyone had been assigned to a breakout group for personal connection time to "share your heart." The room number of each person's group was listed on the back of his name tag. After the emotional display they just sat through, few knew what would be required of them when they were forced to sit down with a group of strangers. For many of the guys it was too much for one night, and many slipped out the side doors to make a quick exit while the groups were assembling.

Obviously, this men's event wasn't built as a station to get curious men to take a ride on a train. It wasn't planned based on the reality of where the men were on their journeys coming into a first-time event. Instead, it awkwardly tried to force strangers into vulnerable, emotional intimacy in a mere couple of hours. As it turned out, it didn't even succeed in getting men to come to the next event, and the program collapsed.

While a nonstop church concentrates on constants and neglects waypoints, and a hyped-up church does the reverse, what I call a *ho-hum church* lacks quality and coordination in both its constants and its waypoints (if they even exist). The church experience feels like "business as usual" with little or limited vibrancy, excitement, or growth. Ministries and programs generally do their own thing with staff not seeing how things fit together or why they're doing certain things versus others. Seemingly positive moments are fleeting. Typically, ho-hum churches experience loss of momentum and steadily decline leaving smaller and smaller numbers of people to wonder "what happened?"

Designing a Church for Breakthrough

A *breakthrough church*, on the other hand, excels in its emphasis on both waypoints and constants to intentionally connect them to one another in clear, meaningful ways. In a breakthrough church, inspiring stations lead people onto effective trains that take them to the destinations of maturity in Christ and kingdom impact that the church has defined in its journey outcomes. This powerful intentionality is the essence of connectivity.

FOUR KINDS OF CHURCHES

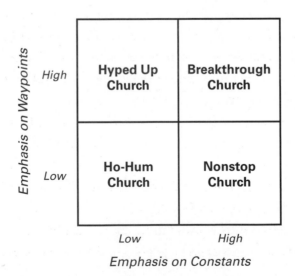

In actual practice, travelers cycle over time between stations (waypoints) and trains (constants). For example, imagine that an enriching event for married couples (waypoint) inspires a struggling couple to participate in an ongoing group that is presently studying the Bible on the topic of building a stronger marriage (constant). After attending the group for several weeks and building relational trust with the leader, the leader refers the couple to a marriage counselor trusted by the church (waypoint), who in turn motivates them to adopt a new, godly practice in their relationship (constant).

The back-and-forth between constants and waypoints, particularly when they are arranged with great intentionality according to the discovered discipleship needs of the people, facilitates personal breakthrough on a wide scale, not just a success story here or there. You can almost hear the *chugga-chugga* of smoothly running trains moving between stations to wonderful destinations instead of the *chug-screech-bam!* of trains that may start suddenly, jerk to a halt, derail, or even collide with each other.

To repeat, constants and waypoints in a breakthrough church are not effective merely because they are individually well-planned and well-run (although they certainly need to be). Rather, breakthrough happens because *each plays its proper role based on its connection to the others.*

I can illustrate with an example from my family. I was a so-so athlete growing up. The main thing that commended me to coaches was my size—I was taller and sturdier than most of my teammates, so I made a decent offensive tackle in youth football mainly because I was good at getting in people's way. My dad, on the other hand, was a terrific natural athlete. When he grew up, he was a star and team captain of every sport he played. As a high school point guard, he was a finalist for the Indiana Mr. Basketball award. (If you know anything about high school basketball in Indiana, you know what a big deal that is.) He was recruited to be the starting point guard at the University of Houston with future NBA legends Elvin Hayes and Don Chaney. If you're a fan of college basketball, you might remember the legendary Houston-UCLA rivalry in the late 1960s that many say put March Madness on the map. Decades later, people in Houston and Indiana still recognize my dad and call on him to be part of sports radio panels and other experiences for "all-time greats." You can tell I love to brag on him.

My dad was a great basketball player, but his value to the team did not come primarily from what he could do on his own as a ballhandler, scorer, passer, and defender. Instead, it came from how well he knew and played his particular role on the team. He was a stellar point guard, which gave him specific duties like bringing the ball up the court, reading the defense, calling the offensive plays, and either scoring himself or feeding the ball with precision to teammates in a good position to score. In other words, he wasn't a strong player just because he was good at what he did in general. He was good at the particular things he was called upon to do, and he knew exactly how his role connected with the particular roles of the other four men on the floor.

Church leaders must have the same sharp awareness of the roles every ministry or program in the church plays—what each is intended to accomplish, what each is *not* intended to accomplish, and how they all explicitly connect to and complement one another.

For instance, almost every church has some version of group ministries that consist of smaller clusters of people than the large-group worship gathering. Leaders commonly believe it's very important to get people into some kind of group, but are they clear and aligned on exactly why it's so important? For the groups at your church, try this thought exercise with your leadership team as an initial experiment.

Step 1. Take ten to fifteen minutes for each member of the team on their own to brainstorm a detailed list of *all* of the aims of various groups in your church. (Namely, why have groups? What are all the specific things they're actually doing or are supposed to accomplish?)

Step 2. Once everyone has written their list, ask them to share with the team everything they wrote (no changes based on what they hear from others). Take turns listening to what each person wrote and capture what everyone says in a list on a whiteboard or flip chart. It might be a fairly long list, which is okay for the purposes of the exercise. If more than one person says the same thing, just keep a tally beside that one bullet (but first make sure the person truly meant the exact same thing; if it meant something different to them—even slightly different—add the extra idea to the compiled list).

Step 3. After you've finished the compilation, facilitate discussion using these suggested questions:

Are the roles and expected aims for our groups clear? Are all our leaders able to articulate the same aims in a specific, concise way?

Is it possible for any single group to accomplish all the aims we've listed? If so, how? If not, why not?

What skills would a group leader need to lead a group that accomplishes all of our aims? Would requiring these skills of every leader assist a multiplying disciple-making movement or hamper it? Why or why not?

Which journey outcomes and outcome expressions do our current groups actively lead people to? Are any of the other aims we've listed distracting groups from shepherding people to these outcomes?

Do all of the outcomes happen in a person's life at the same time shotgun-style, or do some more naturally lead to others over time? Why do you think that is?

Could outcomes be shepherded better in our groups if we clarified and focused the aims of our overall group ministry and/or re-defined how other constants and waypoints connected to our groups? If so, how? If not, why not?

After this conversation, you'll likely have a better idea of where your groups ministry may have opportunities to improve. You probably have groups that accomplish some things, other groups that accomplish others, and maybe some that don't accomplish much. By subsequently prioritizing and aligning what your church's groups are actually supposed to accomplish—with clear definitions—you'll be able to thoughtfully consider what kinds of new waypoints and constants will be most effective in supporting them to achieve the larger purposes. In other words, you'll be able to appropriately subdivide and make clear the particular role that each step of ministry activity should play in the progression of helping people grow in outcome expressions on their journey. You'll also begin to estimate the distance between that ideal and your present reality.

Moving from a definition of the ideal to leading the reality toward the ideal is a big job. But you're not ready to take it on until you consider the rest of the church's ministries as well, because remember: you're trying to move ministry away from disconnected activities to an *integrated* system that your people feel connects well to where they are. So imagine what you would see if, over time, your leadership team walked through *every* ministry area and activity in the church, both constants and waypoints, and you lined all the conclusions up to compare them. By the end of your analysis, you would be able to see:

- what essential functions of a church are being redundantly duplicated among activities
- what essential functions of a church aren't being covered by *any* activities
- how activities might support each other (both in parallel and sequentially)
- how participants might more logically move from engaging in one activity to engaging in another

In short, your activities would be poised to evolve from being disconnected programs to becoming an integrated system. That's the beginning of breakthrough, because you've started minding the connectivity gap.

Connectivity Thinking

Remember, the connectivity gap is the gap between misconnected steps or ministries in your church that short-circuits their
effectiveness. You might wonder why I emphasize the term *connec-*
tivity over *connection* or *connecting*. While the latter terms are very
common in the digital age and certainly in churches, they are used
so expansively, even cavalierly, that their meaning can be lost or mis-
understood—kind of like the word *love* that can so easily be applied
to a range of meanings. The definition of *connectivity* provides a
deeper picture of the breakthrough integration I'm espousing.
Connectivity is the seamless flow of multiple integrated connections
through which an entire system oper-
ates. In other words, the term *connec-*
tion refers to the *act* of connecting
while the more powerful "connectivity" is the state of *being* connected
interdependently. Leaders who are
minding the connectivity gap are
continually giving thoughtful attention to how the entire system is inter-
connected, not just running around plugging and unplugging a lot
of connections.

> Connection is the act of connecting. Connectivity is the state of *being* connected interdependently.

Regardless of where churches are when they start the journey,
this way of thinking helps them break through to deeper levels of
integration according to the realities of their context. Building off
our last exercise, here's an example from one church on that journey
with a problem that might seem familiar. The church had a persis-
tent issue with determining its best model for groups, and it never
seemed to get resolved.

Over the years, the church tried a variety of different formats at different times. They tried big groups, small groups, men's groups, women's groups, multigenerational groups, topical groups, and everything in between. They changed the name of the groups and group ministry, launching and relaunching them in a number of ways. (A running joke of lay leaders was "I wonder what we're going to call our groups this month.") Although a reasonable number of people participated, group growth across the church hadn't significantly improved and the church longed for a much higher percentage of regular attenders to engage. Once again, they found the discussion reemerging.

At this point in the game, the church was offering mid-size Bible study groups on Sundays and a variety of smaller and topical groups in homes and other locations throughout the week. Some leaders felt that the church's program structure was too unwieldy, required too much collective energy, and confused attenders about their next step. They viewed the Sunday morning offerings as part of the problem, and wanted to do away with them in favor of putting all the energy and attention on midweek small groups meeting in homes. Part of the rationale was they felt small groups in homes achieved greater transparency and intimacy which, to those leaders, was the most important purpose of groups.

On the other side, some leaders felt that Sunday mid-size groups should be preserved. They believed they were beneficial to the growth of many attenders and that many wouldn't migrate to small home groups as a replacement, diminishing their involvement. They thought God had wired many people to more naturally connect in mid-size gatherings at first, which then would organically lead to transparent relationships in microgroups. As such, they suspected there was deeper discipleship happening than was readily apparent but didn't know for sure. They wanted to keep the Sunday groups going but clearly distinguish them from small groups, putting each ministry in its own category with distinctly different purposes.

The church eventually realized that its biggest problem was that *leaders had been debating models instead of discerning outcomes* and they needed to embark on a journey seeking God's wisdom for the very purpose of the ministry. After significant thoughtful dialogue, prayer, and reflection, the church arrived at a solution that wasn't win-lose or even a compromise but rather demonstrated a process of arriving at true integration. Without even looking at the current or prior group structures—which sometimes took discipline to avoid—leaders clearly and concisely defined what they expected all groups to accomplish in participants' lives based on the church's newly defined journey outcomes. This led them down a road to prioritize groups not as a place that just *contributed* to discipleship, but that became the *disciple-making hub for the entire church.*

> Debating models won't help until you've investigated your church's outcomes.

This provided remarkable freedom in the way they approached organizing the groups. Because the leaders had arrived at a clear articulation of new expectations for all groups, they could look at the structure with fresh eyes. They realized that size, location, and day of the week weren't nearly so important as the training they as staff leaders provided to volunteer group leaders to achieve the expectations. In other words, they realized they needed to capture and reorient the group leaders' minds and hearts around the greater mission of discipling people in the journey outcomes instead of only focusing on whatever they happened to think their group was supposed to be doing before. This meant group leaders would become on-the-ground partners with staff (or "metapartners," as I'll describe in chapter 9) to discern whether what was happening was actually moving the needle in people's lives or not.

For example, one of the church's journey outcomes was "How am I connecting on a deeper level with my Life Group?" with six specific outcome expressions that group leaders were trained to facilitate such as "I share in the personal joys and challenges of the people in my Life Group" and "My Life Group helps me to seek ways to build intentional relationships with non-Christians. This could happen in a variety of ways and would unfold differently in different groups, but the staff's role became to consistently check in with group leaders on what was working or not and provide them with coaching and creative resources based on the unique size, makeup, and journey progress of the people in each group.

The church rebranded Sunday midsize gatherings and small midweek home gatherings under the same umbrella. This simplified people's next step in choosing a weekly group that fit their schedule, preferred demographic, or style of connecting. People were able to engage in whichever alternative felt right to them, but wherever they went and whenever it was held, they entered a group tailored to meet the same objectives.

This was reinforced by the way the learning content of all Life Groups was designed and subsequently promoted in worship gatherings. One of the four stated expectations of all groups was "Study: Learning to apply God's Word from the weekly messages." So in every sermon every week, the pastor would plan a way to casually but directly introduce the compelling topic all Life Groups would be discussing in their next weekly meeting. For example, he would say something like, "Hey, in your Life Groups this next week you're going to be talking more about this idea of [insert scintillating topic here that the pastor had wryly set up in his sermon]." It should be noted that the group content wasn't discussion about the sermon itself, but built off a key idea that connected to the sermon without rehashing it.

Once the church began living out this consistent connectivity and two-way communication, group participation doubled in a single ministry season (less than four months). It had taken a lot of intentional thinking and work to reach this focus in their group ministry, but the result was a path that facilitated people's next moves with Christ, energized participants, and delivered much deeper formative experiences over the long haul. It worked because it uniquely fit their culture, wasn't copied and pasted from someone else, and directly began addressing their awareness and connectivity gaps.

Here's an example of a different church that thoughtfully moved another ministry toward deeper connectivity. In the previous chapter I told you about a church that misjudged the impact of choosing to dissolve their church's men's ministry, then after a number of years unsuccessfully tried to restart it with an ill-conceived event. So, there still was no men's ministry though it was a definite need based on the deeper disciple-making outcomes the church was developing. After more years went by, it tried to revive the ministry again, but this time with a new plan that skillfully integrated and balanced varying group sizes.

The core of the new ministry was a semester-based weekly Bible study held at the church. When people arrived, they gathered in consistent small groups sitting around the same tables to reconnect personally, build community, and discuss the substantial homework they completed on their own the week before. Then midway through the gathering, a leader taught on the passage, instantly transforming the space into a large group gathering. The teaching depth was especially compelling because it didn't color the perspectives of people in the room before each person had an opportunity to study and discuss what the Spirit was showing them individually. Midsize serving opportunities in the community were also offered, allowing multiple small groups to organically build deeper relationships with others.

Leaders of the ministry kept in close touch with small group leaders in a checkup loop to keep their finger on the pulse of what was happening in the ministry. The relaunch of the ministry was so successful that it eventually became a fire hazard to cram more round tables into the big room.

Before restarting, this church had a seemingly simple ministry structure primarily focused on worship, small groups, and missions opportunities—with most ministry functions relegated to isolated small groups. But leaders began to realize something was missing based on their newly emerging outcomes. So, they skillfully designed a men's ministry that combined large group teaching, small group connecting, and midsize group serving in one package that felt seamless to participants. This transformed it from a shallow ministry strategy to a deeper experience that was far more growth-oriented for the men involved—though quite sophisticated behind the scenes to implement with excellence.

Again, this worked because it fit the unique culture and context of that particular church, and reflected greater emphasis on overcoming prior awareness and connectivity gaps in the ministry that was relaunched. It also revealed a fresh willingness to innovate, test, and improve as it launched the various stages of the new ministry.

The *way of thinking* that these examples illustrate is what all churches can and should reach for on the road to connectivity. If the journey your attenders take today feels as disconnected as being stranded on the tarmac in St. Louis or as haphazard as taking four flights and seventeen and a half hours to get to Des Moines, you can convert it into an experience that makes a genuine impact in people's lives to bring them closer and closer to Christ. Leadership is about doing the hard but exhilarating work to arrive at the kind of ministry connectivity that powerfully grows your people from wherever they are to wherever God calls them to be. And you'll know it's happening based on real outcomes that can be discerned and celebrated.

We've been focusing intently on the integration of church activities and the connectivity between them because these subjects are so often neglected. Doing this with depth reminds us how important it is to reorient our thinking to see everything a church does as a system. That frees us to evaluate and make useful, informed adjustments to what we're currently doing. As we showed in the last example, that is not to say that individual ministries themselves are unimportant. A breakthrough ministry system is always composed of excellent parts. So in the next two chapters we turn our attention to what makes a great constant and what makes a great waypoint, both what they have in common and how each excels in its own way.

{ CHAPTER 7 }

Waypoints and Constants, Part 1: Five Tests for Every Ministry

If you ever wonder whether God cares about systems," I heard a pastor say, "just look up at the stars." "Can you fasten the chains of the Pleiades or loosen the belt of Orian?" God asked Job. "Can you bring out the constellations in their season and lead the Bear and her cubs? Do you know the laws of heaven? Can you impose its authority on earth?" (Job 38:31–33). God created systems in an inconceivable universe of a hundred billion galaxies of about a hundred million stars apiece that we can presently see, not to mention those we never will. And they all move in a regular dance that moves impossibly fast while the positions of the partners change extraordinarily slowly. "The heavens declare the glory of God, and the sky above proclaims his handiwork," David says (Ps. 19:1 ESV).

The celestial realm displays God's love of systems, but how much more the system of a living creature. "For it was you who created my inward parts," David sang. "[Y]ou knit me together in my mother's womb. I will praise you because I have been remarkably and wondrously made" (Ps. 139:13–14). Just take a moment and look at your hand. Flex it; spread your fingers and contract them again; move them one at a time. Imagine all that has to work right to make a simple gesture that you do without thinking every day—the perfect alignment of bones, tendons, ligaments, muscles, and skin; the nerves that feel and generate movement faster than the speed of thought; the blood that carries nutrients to the cells; the organelles within cells that metabolize the latent energy to exert force, that repair themselves, that reproduce to build back stronger after strain. All of it in a healthy hand composes a perfectly arranged system, yet it isn't independent, for it only makes up a small portion of the whole system of the human body.

And as much as we can see God's love of systems in a living creature, we can see so much more in the complex relationship between all living creatures from the tallest tree to the tiniest microorganism in an ecosystem, perfectly balanced, perfectly adapted to its climate and geology as an awesome diversity of life that sustains itself and is sustained by soil, air, and water. Each ecosystem is interdependent with every other ecosystem to form an entire, integrated, interpenetrating globe of life that shapes and is shaped by the contours of land and sea. The connectivity is awe-inspiring.

In every chapter of this book, I can't stress enough the importance of system and connectivity in the life of the church, because it reflects how God made everything to work. I also stress the systemic nature of things because paying attention to it doesn't come easily, and it's often neglected in how we do ministry.

I also emphasize the importance of systems here because it's critical to interpret this chapter in that light. For a moment, I want to turn our view from the overall system of ministry to the components that compose that system. These components either bring connectivity to that system or don't, depending on how we as leaders design them and interact with them. Continuing with the analogy of the Underground, we're going to look at the stations (called waypoints) and trains (called constants) that make up the disciple-making system of the church. Though we must never forget that breakthrough comes out of the integration of all the parts, we also have to design the parts well so that they integrate with the others. This chapter lays out foundational design principles that should apply to everything you're operating in your church in a breakthrough system of connectivity.

To begin, we must make a clear delineation between the *process* of ministry design and the way we *evaluate* that design through quality control criteria.

To clarify the difference, let's think about a topic near to my heart (and stomach)—barbecue. While I can appreciate the lesser contributions of chicken, pork, and turkey to this revered cuisine, I don't hesitate to call expertly smoked brisket the most succulent meat in the world. And of all pitmasters, one of the greatest anywhere might be a legendary Austin, Texas, chef named Aaron Franklin. Franklin has built a national reputation bordering on sacred using detailed methods that let him know everything that's going on inside his cooker. He smokes his brisket for fifteen hours using a process that requires constant attention and precision.

Written out, Franklin's elaborate brisket recipe is nearly twelve pages long.

But Franklin's process—the recipe—isn't the same as his standards of quality. Franklin has specific criteria for three different parts of brisket: the fat, the flat (the main meaty part), and the point (fatty muscle that sits on top of the flat). Each carries its own expectations for appearance, taste, and texture—from moistness and flavor infusion to the smoke ring and critical brick-black bark. These are examples of quality control criteria. They aren't the way to cook brisket; they define what brisket is supposed to be like once it's cooked.[1]

In a similar way, I will present reflective criteria for ministries, the aspects by which we can judge ministry design. Just as appearance, taste, and texture apply to the fat, the flat, and the point of brisket, in the same way the criteria I offer here apply to every different kind of church engagement in their own way. They apply to big group engagements like worship services, mid-sized groups, small groups, and microgroups. They apply to ministries to seniors, to median adults, to young adults, to students, and to children. They apply to study, service, support, and song. To be sure, each specific kind of ministry has its own unique characteristics, but the criteria I describe here apply in varying ways to all of the activities on your church's calendar.

Whenever effective measurement reveals that a part of the church system isn't working the way it should to grow the outcomes you're seeking in people's lives, these criteria provide a framework

---

1. Steven Raichlen, *The Brisket Chronicles: How to Barbecue, Braise, Smoke, and Cure the World's Most Epic Cut of Meat* (New York: Workman, 2019), 7, 262.

for deeper evaluation to diagnose what's missing or broken. They're also very useful when a new ministry initiative is on the drawing board, because they form the rubric that good design aims for. After all, if enthusiasts find brisket important enough for detailed criteria, how much more important they should be for our effectiveness as leaders of the church!

Remember, this is not about putting God in a box, as the saying goes; it's not about confining his work in people's lives. It's about examining whether the things we as church leaders are doing to cooperate with God in the work he's entrusted to us are truly the best we can do.

To continue with this thought, I want to go deeper into quality control criteria here; in later chapters we'll explore how the process works in more detail with a number of examples.

Quality Control Criteria for All Ministries

As a brief reminder, in chapter 1 I defined two kinds of engagements that churches plan and promote:

1. *Constants* are ongoing engagements—things that people do regularly over an extended period of time. They include both consistent church activities and personal habits of life. They are like trains in the Underground; they enable *perpetual movement* toward destinations (journey outcomes in people's lives).

2. *Waypoints* are one-time or temporary experiences—things like special events, focused campaigns (for example, all groups

centered on the same subject matter for six weeks), and restorative ministries (for example, grief counseling). They are the stations in the Underground, enabling *pivotal moments* where people hop a train to a new destination. In other words, waypoints are where people commit to a new constant that promises growth toward an outcome they're seeking in their life.

Constants and waypoints are the building blocks of an integrated ministry system. Each has its own role to play, but they have much in common as well. Accordingly, I'd like to present eleven quality control criteria in three groups. I call these criteria "tests."

Both constants and waypoints can be evaluated by:

- the empathy test
- the proximity test
- the totality test
- the variability test
- the spirituality test

Waypoints are also evaluated by:

- the curiosity test
- the potentiality test
- the continuity test

Constants are also evaluated by:

- the intentionality test
- the vitality test
- the expectancy test

This might seem like a lot at first, but don't worry—you can handle this! The tests unlock significant thoughtful perspective on evaluation and breakthrough. They point you to specific places to look whenever you want to examine a ministry's effectiveness more deeply. As you get comfortable with them, it will get easier and easier to quickly recognize them in action and see where greater attention to one or more of them is needed in certain ministries.

In this chapter, we'll examine the five tests for both constants and waypoints; then in the next chapter we'll look at the three focused tests specific to waypoints and the three for constants. But before we get ahead of ourselves, I don't want to give you the wrong impression. These aren't the only standards for doing something in your church. You already have trains running, and you probably have stations too. These criteria are primarily meant to help you take a closer look at what you have. A train might look good at a distance, for instance, but on closer inspection it has lots of issues. Perhaps its day is done and it's time to throw it on the scrap heap, or it might just need to go into the shop for repairs—maybe for something as simple as a tune-up or new coat of paint. The tests point you to places to look more carefully to determine what might need attention. As you examine a ministry according to these tests, keep an open and flexible mind about the various ways you might get it in top condition for the part it plays in the overall system. And remember, in a system all the tests work together, so just because you're doing well on one test doesn't make something effective if you're failing another one.

The Empathy Test

We'll look at the tests that apply to all ministries before discussing the ones that are specific to waypoints or constants. The first is the empathy test; it asks, **"How well does this show appreciation for where people are when they first engage?"** A waypoint or constant passes the empathy test when a participant's initial experience accommodates their level of knowledge, their acquaintance with others in the room, and their emotional and spiritual state. It fails the empathy test when a participant feels early on that the engagement was meant for someone else, especially someone who is in some way further ahead, so to speak, than they are.

If church leaders ever give serious attention to people's state of heart and mind at the point of initial engagement, it is usually in the context of what's called "guest experience" or "first impressions," to help newcomers to the church's largest gathering—usually Sunday worship—have such a positive experience that they want to come back. There are parts of first impressions ministries that overlap with the empathy test, but what I'm talking about goes much deeper and wider.

The empathy test is deeper because it focuses on the entirety of a person's "point A" from the moment they first become aware of a specific church engagement they might choose to participate in. It isn't mainly about what will make them feel pleased, like receiving a gift. It isn't just about how to get them involved, though that's part of it. Instead, it's about being attentive to where they are or may be intellectually, emotionally, socially, and spiritually and respecting that in how the entire experience is designed.

The empathy test shouldn't be confused with only making people feel comfortable. The purpose isn't to please a customer. Rather, empathy in church leadership is about appreciating and accommodating where a person is starting from in order to lead them deeper with God effectively. It's the recognition that there is no way to get someone to point B without first respecting their point A, however uncomfortable that point A may be. We care about the participant's starting point, not out of concern for what they are pleased by but out of loving anticipation of what God may desire for them to become.

The empathy test was missing in the men's ministry event that I described earlier. When men walked into the big event, they instantly encountered snacks and cornhole. On the surface, that seems like thoughtful, hospitable concern for the newcomer; after all, what guy doesn't enjoy snacks and cornhole? But a little more thought reveals a fairly obvious problem: little boys who don't know each other might spontaneously play together, but grown men usually don't play games with strangers unless that's the expected purpose, like going to the YMCA for a pickup basketball game.

The men's event had features that superficially mimicked hospitality. It lacked empathy, which comes from genuine understanding of what things feel like from the guest's perspective. (The lack of empathy became even more evident in the decisions that led to the main program's steep emotional curve, which also fails some of the other tests to come.)

The empathy test isn't just deeper than first impressions ministry; it's also wider. If churches devote energy to welcoming newcomers as they are, they usually concentrate it on welcoming people to the worship service. But every activity of the church requires the same level of attention. Even if a person has attended church for years, if they go to a particular church activity that they've never attended before, they are a guest there, and they need the experience to be crafted with deep sensitivity to their point A.

The empathy test even applies to individual habits. Think through the practicalities of starting a new, unfamiliar, perhaps uncomfortable routine. If you want people to start a daily Bible reading habit, for example, make sure they have a readable Bible and a functional knowledge of what to expect when they open it, and how to approach the text, because no one is born with this knowledge.[2]

This may initially seem like common sense, but in the vast majority of churches it isn't commonly applied across their ministries with the necessary attention and depth.

The Proximity Test

The second test of constants and waypoints is the proximity test. It asks, **"How well does your space and intimacy design match with participants' willingness to get close?"** The constant or waypoint passes the proximity test when the physical environment, social environment, and prompting by leaders coaxes an appropriate level of participation and open disclosure without people feeling forced. It fails the test when leaders ask people to engage or share more openly (or leaders share more themselves) than the environment allows or when an environment suitable for intimacy is wasted on less intimate moments.

The field of proxemics provides great resources to help in applying this test. Proxemics is a study of the different physical distances

2. For more on cultivating biblical literacy, see Jen Wilkin, *Women of the Word: How to Study the Bible with Both Our Hearts and Our Minds* (Wheaton, IL: Crossway, 2014).

between people that facilitate different kinds of communication, from public to social to personal to intimate. These levels of distance correspond to the number of people who can share that kind of communication together at one time, and it also connects with the dimensions of enclosed spaces where communication happens.

Churches bump into proxemics problems all the time. For instance, a church with a hundred people in the room on a Sunday morning is at a continual disadvantage when it tries to lead worship with people seated in rows. It's trying to pull off public communication with a social-sized group. It gets even worse when the hundred are sitting in a room that seats four hundred. The space itself screams that it is made for a public event three to four times that size, but without that many present, the intangible quality of good public communication is always missing. Small churches get stuck in the trap of people not showing up to their public event because there aren't enough people at their public event.

Similarly, leaders of large churches usually come to accept that there rarely will be much real personal contact at a worship service except perhaps for conversations before or after the event between people who are acquainted already. To facilitate greater intimacy, then, these churches might run small groups that meet in the personal space of someone's living room. So to make it easier on leaders, churches often distribute prepackaged content so that all leaders have to do is press play on a video and then read a set of questions. But this actually forces *public* communication (the video) into *personal* space; this can be especially problematic for videos that literally show a preacher or teacher talking to a big audience. So, unless a group's leader is especially skilled at cultivating a personal space that deepens growth, the small group might not really complement weekend worship; it might just be repeating the public gathering concept all over again in the potentially awkward setting of someone's home. I'm not saying the speaker-to-large-group video can't work sometimes, but if public communication in a personal space is your default approach, you probably aren't maximizing the opportunity.

I could keep going, but the point is that to pass the proximity test, be sure to first identify the degree of personal intimacy that best facilitates the clearly defined purpose of the activity. That will determine how many and the profile of leaders you need, how you need to train them in advance, how large the space you employ should be, how you subdivide the space (for instance, with round tables instead of rows of chairs), and how you promote the activity to set the right expectations for the people you want to come. Fortunately, multiple resources are available to help leaders apply the principles of proxemics to church ministry.[3]

The Totality Test

The third test for constants and waypoints is the totality test; it asks, **"How well does this both expand the mind and move the heart?"** A constant or waypoint passes the totality test when a participant discovers something new and is moved within to become, do, or continue something in obedience to Christ. It fails the test

3. Bobby Harrington and Alex Absalom, *Discipleship That Fits: The Five Kinds of Relationships God Uses to Help Us Grow* (Grand Rapids: Zondervan, 2016); Neil Cole, *Church 3.0: Upgrades for the Future of the Church* (San Francisco: Jossey-Bass, 2010), 139–59.

when a participant receives content without feeling anything or experiences emotion without learning anything.

I'm not suggesting that there aren't environments or experiences that lean more toward thinking or feeling. Clearly, some will. However, if teaching is not substantive enough to ever stir any sense of feeling or if emotional environments consistently lack substance, something is missing. The totality test refers to the totality of the human person. Human beings have intellects and emotions. No one can become fully conformed to the likeness of Christ—the goal of discipleship—unless both the intellect and emotions are transformed to think as Christ thinks and feel as Christ feels. A disciple without a Christlike mind may have the purest intentions, but without the wisdom to understand the scope and detail of what reality is and what it should be, they're liable to be ineffective and sometimes harmful when they try to do good. On the other hand, a disciple without a Christlike heart may have a clear perspective and sound doctrine, but without reordered motivations that love what Christ loves and hate what he hates, they'll struggle to resist temptation and to take action to love others.

It's easy to agree with this concept in principle, but harder to put into practice. Many churches and many church leaders are a good deal more comfortable with intellect than they are with emotion or vice versa. Whatever lip-service they pay to the need for both, it comes naturally to prioritize one over the other in ministry design and evaluation according to their unconscious preference.

As a quick, rough self-diagnostic, try to think of all the churches, denominations, traditions, and cultures that are more emotional than your church and then all the ones that are more intellectual. If the length of your lists is imbalanced, your church probably is too.

Another way to check for imbalance is to explore what you think *must* happen in every ministry activity you do or else "church" hasn't really happened for you. Is it Bible study (intellectual) or is it music (emotional)? Is it prayer that rearticulates the faith (intellectual) or prayer that elicits shouts of affirmation (emotional)? Is it a conclusion with next steps (intellectual) or one with hugs (emotional)?

Churches must pursue finding a balance between expanding the mind and moving the heart. Doing this allows you to touch the range of people God has given you to reach. You might have a specific mission field consisting of a neighborhood or an unreached people group, but I doubt God has given you a mission field consisting of just one personality type!

It takes proactive effort to ensure that activities feed both the mind and the heart. As I alluded to earlier, in this case it's acceptable if some of your engagements lean one way or the other within reason as long as your ministry system as a whole passes the totality test.

The Variability Test

The fourth test that applies to constants and waypoints alike is the variability test. This one asks, **"How well do we vary the intensity and type of communicated emotion in this?"** This test applies less to an individual constant or waypoint than it does to all of them taken as a whole (though individual constants and waypoints still should be evaluated for this). Your constants and waypoints pass the variability test when they express the breadth of your people's emotional responses to life and when a balanced mix of them are highly emotional, low-key, and in between. This is different from the totality test that emphasizes the balance of mind and heart. Instead, the variability test focuses on the degree and kind of emotion expressed representing the range of human experience.

When comparing the intensity and type of emotion, think about the difference between a radio's volume knob and tuning knob. With the *volume* knob, you dial the intensity up and down to fit the situation; there's a big difference between soft background music to accompany a conversation over an intimate dinner and cranking it up full blast in a convertible with the top down. Likewise, the emotional intensity of some engagements should be loud and others soft, and all should have some variation between the two over the course of the time spent together. Louds aren't really loud without the softs, and vice versa, whether in music or speaking. If everything you do is exciting, it's probably just noisy. And if everything you do is tranquil, it's likely just boring. The same "volume" principle applies to lighting. Greater emotional connection comes from *variance* in lighting. For example, there may be reflective or hushed moments of worship and prayer that call for lights in the room to be dimmed, but then increased brightly for more majestic moments or during speaking. I've had a number of church leaders chuckle (or gasp) over the years upon realizing that the "intimacy" they were trying to create by keeping the lights low during the whole worship service actually lulled some people to sleep while others who were trying to take notes or read their Bibles along with Scripture readings literally couldn't see. God has given us amazingly perceptive senses of vision and hearing that help people connect with him and his creativity when we remember to carefully build in a full range of expression with our volume knob.

Using your ministry design *tuning* knob, on the other hand, you vary the *type* of emotion. Are there engagements in your church with exuberant joy? What about awe? How about emotions that make us uncomfortable, like sadness, fear, and even holy anger at times? The Psalms indicate that these were all part of the gathered worship of ancient Israel, with unshakable faith in God undergirding all of it. Do your ministries vary emotional tone to span the dial of human experience?

The Spirituality Test

The final test that applies to both constants and waypoints is the spirituality test. This test pertains specifically to the ones where participants are serving, not receiving. It asks, **"How well does this disciple people spiritually as they serve?"** A constant or waypoint passes the spirituality test when participants are consciously connected to the spiritual dimension of the activity and are being developed in faith and love as they serve. It fails when the activity is fixated on accomplishment and performance because leaders don't adequately engage participants in conversations and practices that help them grow as disciples.

An example of the spirituality test involves two choirs in two churches that I experienced. One choir was led by a professional musician who was a skilled director. Choir members were volunteers who attended the church and had a love for or background in music. The group had a good selection of music, and practices were run efficiently. The choir was well prepared to sing, and it enhanced the worship service when they did.

The other choir also was led by an excellent director. The volunteers loved to sing and enjoyed experiencing God's presence through a wide range of worshipful music as they served in the choir. Rehearsals were well planned, and the choir's musical excellence added much to the flow of worship gatherings.

But there was more. The second leader opened every weekly rehearsal with a time of worship so choir members could unwind from their workweeks and reorient their tightened or tired spirits, souls, and bodies in praise to the Lord. He shared words from Scripture and encouraging testimonies about God's faithfulness, how God was using each person in the choir to minister, and gave biblical context for both the sermon series and specific songs that were going to be rehearsed. He sprinkled in stories of the origins of hymns and praise choruses to give extra meaning to each one's significance, power, and planned role within each worship gathering. He intentionally discipled people in what having a posture of worship meant not just when the choir was gathered but in their lives every day. The group was given time every week to build relationships and share what was going on in their lives. People knew each others' names and gregariously welcomed and introduced newcomers to the ministry. They got to know one another, prayed together, supported one another during times of struggle, and held each other accountable to their daily responsibility as worship leaders and worship disciplers. This responsibility lived itself out across the church as hundreds of well-equipped choir members modeled and shared the meaning of lifestyle worship in their small groups, mid-size groups, and other areas where they served. The whole choir would sometimes get together to serve the community and other times would gather for fun and fellowship. And when it came time to sing in worship, a high expectation was given to spiritual preparation to give God the glory with him alone as the audience, setting the tone and blazing the path for the rest of the congregation to join the consistently growing group in vibrant worship every week.

Both choirs were excellent musically, but the latter passed the spirituality test while the former did not.

There is one other important detail we should note about the two choirs. The first one, despite its excellence and the genuine desire of people to participate at first, never seemed to last. It would get going for a while, and then people would drift away, bowing out, and the choir would cease. Then, it would start up again, run for a while, and collapse like the time before. The church eventually decided to plan on the choir just getting together every quarter or so, with hurried rehearsals to get the music ready for the weekend. This only worsened the problem due to the lack of consistent relational connection and absence of intentional discipleship. People literally didn't know one another and relationships weren't cultivated as part of a mobilized ministry in any way. They weren't discipled toward any clear outcomes related to worship, just toward duty. They felt pressure during choir rehearsals to learn the music quickly because they only had a few rehearsals when reassembled. Many said they felt intimidated because even though they loved worship, music, and singing, they didn't have enough musical experience to keep up when rehearsals were sporadic and limited to a relatively short amount of time. And because people weren't introduced to one another, let alone welcomed into a relational group with a meaningful mission, it felt like no one knew or cared if they were even there or not. Sadly, what started as an eager group of 150 dwindled to just 10 a few times a year. At one point, the church's lead pastor even publicly expressed that when the choir would start meeting, the members generally wouldn't stick with it to keep it going, with the clear implication that the choir's inconsistency was the participants' fault. The leaders weren't seeing or owning that it was actually their fault.

By contrast, the second choir was and still is consistent and robust in their role as "24/7 worship disciplers" throughout the church. Participants made it a priority in their lives and could hardly wait for each week's rehearsal gathering. It was a strong spiritual community integrated and connected within the larger community of the church, and people who were part of it almost always remained committed.

The difference was that the leader—the pastor—of the second choir didn't see his job as preparing music for an upcoming worship event. He saw his job as pastoring and discipling the flock that was his for a few hours each week to serve and disciple the rest of the congregation throughout the year. He and others in the group used the serving activity every week as a vehicle for training a family of disciplers in the area of worship. Because of this, the choir met every week consistently throughout the year, building relationship and growing in personal worship-related outcomes together regardless of their singing schedule. The leader didn't choose between musical excellence and spiritual growth; his efforts bore both liturgical and spiritual fruit.

The spiritual test reminds us that everything—literally everything—in a God-honoring church should be about making disciples. No activity or gathering is left out. Leaders see to it that even those who are serving are also growing and sharing that growth with more and more people in creative ways.

CHAPTER 8

Waypoints and Constants, Part 2: What Makes Pivotal Moments and Perpetual Movement

N ow that we've explored the tests that apply to all church engage-ments, let's shift our focus to three tests that apply specifically to waypoints, the stations in the Underground that inspire pivotal moments in people's lives. But before we do so, it's important to understand that there's more to the difference between waypoints and constants than just how long they run. Yes, waypoints are one-time or temporary experiences and constants are ongoing engage-ments (the trains that enable perpetual movement), but they differ in their characteristics, not just in duration.

Focused Quality Control Criteria for Waypoints

I can illustrate the difference with a story that Malcolm Gladwell tells in his book *Blink* about the legendary product flop called New Coke.[1] In the 1980s, Pepsi made a new, aggressive push to gain market share from Coca-Cola, especially among young people. Pepsi branded itself "the choice of a new generation" and signed pop phenomenon Michael Jackson to star in its television ads. But perhaps Pepsi's biggest threat to Coke came from a side-by-side, blind taste test called the Pepsi Challenge. At malls and shopping centers around the country, a shopper would be offered a sip of Pepsi and a sip of Coke without knowing which was which. Once they named their preference and were told which drink they selected, many were surprised to learn they had picked Pepsi. In fact, an overwhelming majority of Americans favored Pepsi over Coke.

Coke viewed this as a serious threat to its market dominance over all generations, not just younger people, so Coke reformulated its recipe to compete. In 1985, with great fanfare, the company relaunched its signature product with the new recipe, known colloquially as New Coke.

New Coke *bombed*. It wasn't that everyone hated it; many were pleased. But many were not. Those who didn't like the change—especially in the South, where Coke was a matter of regional pride—were extremely vocal about it. I remember going to a Houston Astros game in those days, and when a commercial for New Coke was shown on the screens, the whole stadium booed—and booed loudly!

---

1. Malcolm Gladwell, *Blink: The Power of Thinking without Thinking* (New York: Little, Brown and Company, 2005), 157–67.

In only three months, Coca-Cola started selling its traditional recipe again under the name Coca-Cola Classic, and sales rapidly rebounded. In 1992 the company rebranded New Coke as "Coke II" before phasing it out entirely ten years later.

But this isn't the end of the story; there's a critical additional point that many people are not aware of. Gladwell points out that the Pepsi Challenge actually stacked the deck in favor of Pepsi, not because the company lied about tasters' preferences (it didn't) but because of the nature of Pepsi itself. Pepsi is a bit sweeter and smoother than Coke. When you compare the two drinks sip for sip, as in the taste test, Pepsi is more sippable. But Coke is a bit drier with a characteristic bite that many find more enjoyable over a whole bottle. Pepsi initially *seemed* better than Coke not because it was better in general but because it was better for a Dixie cup, not for a tall glass.

In ministry design, you can compare waypoints to Pepsi and constants to Coke. Waypoints need to be smooth and sweet; they need to move someone in a short amount of time, but they aren't an experience a person would want every week. Constants, on the other hand, need to be more drinkable over the long haul, more complex with a bit more bite that grows on you over time. They are to be engagements that you come back to again and again, and they continue to delight.

The Curiosity Test

In light of this, as we discuss the focused tests for waypoints, it makes sense that the first criterion is the curiosity test. It asks, **"How well does this grab people's attention so that they want to know more?"** A waypoint passes the curiosity test when people are leaning in with eagerness to learn, experience, or participate. It fails the test when people's interest wanes or isn't caught to begin with because there's nothing out of the ordinary in what's being offered to them.

A waypoint can't be boring. It can never be same old, same old. It has to be novel, interesting, fascinating. Even if it's an event that happens repeatedly at certain junctures (like an annual holiday service), it only needs to take place every once in a while so that people are ready to experience it again when it comes around. And still, it shouldn't be exactly the same as it was the time before.

The curiosity test applies in two phases, the first being the promotion of the waypoint. The name, activity, and subject matter need to be compelling all by themselves so that even if you have almost no time to explain it, people will instantly want to know more. But the curiosity test also applies to the experience itself. If the waypoint is a special event, it should continually unfold. There should be surprise, mystery, intrigue. A person shouldn't be so startled that they're upset, but they also shouldn't be able to predict everything that's going to happen between the welcome and the dismissal.

The curiosity test doesn't only apply to special events and focused campaigns, however. It also applies to restorative ministries that meet new needs that people become aware of in their lives. In those situations, the curiosity isn't driven by savvy promotion or clever naming; to the contrary, people in distress don't want something that feels exciting but something that feels very safe. Instead, curiosity comes from the need that has been awakened in the person. For example, a church might quietly host a support group for the bereaved for years, and some people would have no curiosity about it. But if one of those same people were to lose their spouse, they would suddenly become much more curious.

This example also touches on an important point: different people get curious about different things. A grief support group and a special event involving a live elephant both elicit curiosity, but not from the same people or for the same reason. Over the course of a ministry's whole calendar, leaders need to be acutely aware that different personality types are intrigued by very different things. Some like exciting; some like thoughtful. Some like warm; some like intense. In fact, there's someone in your church— more importantly, someone who is friends with someone in your church—whose curiosity is aroused by something that you personally find totally uninteresting. Are you savvy enough in your thinking and research to design waypoints to reach that person?

> Different personality types are intrigued by very different things.

The Potentiality Test

The second test of a waypoint is the potentiality test; it asks, **"How well does this focus people's attention on a potential outcome for their life?"** A waypoint passes the potentiality test when it raises people's awareness, understanding, and appreciation of a journey outcome to the point where they want to take a next step. It fails the test when it is disconnected from any outcome or when it scatters people's attention among many so that people aren't motivated to do anything different as a result of the experience.

In an earlier chapter I mentioned how the buildings on Main Street at Disney World gradually get shorter as they get nearer to Cinderella's Castle to draw people's attention to that landmark.

The technique is called "forced perspective." I like the concept of "nurtured perspective" to describe how a waypoint directs someone's attention to a particular journey outcome chosen by ministry designers to be the focus.

Of all criteria pertaining to waypoints, this one is probably met the least often. Since most churches have never clearly defined their outcomes, they can't begin to design a waypoint with a specific outcome or outcome expression in mind.

If a journey outcome is authentic and biblical, it will touch a genuine need a person has, *even if that person isn't in Christ yet.* As examples, let's examine a few of the sample outcomes from chapter 3:

> "How am I discovering and developing my unique, God-given purpose?" No one wants to live a purposeless life, and no one wants to believe that they have no value other than as a duplicate of another person. Of course this desire for unique purpose and calling is true of Jesus-followers, but it's also true of everyone. Purpose and worth are universal human needs.

> "How am I being real and accountable in a small group of disciples?" Everyone, believer or nonbeliever, desperately wants to know that they're accepted as they are. In a community survey I did, a person who described himself as a "committed atheist" said that he'd "be willing to consider attending a church group if the people were genuinely friendly and caring." When people are sure they can be real and safe, they become open to engaging

with and even being challenged by the people who accept them. There also are people, both believers and nonbelievers alike, who have goals in life they want to achieve, and they're already looking for people with similar goals who can encourage them with accountability along the way.

"How am I sharing the gospel with people who don't know Jesus?" Is it crazy to think that even a person who isn't following Jesus has an innate need to more deeply explore and perhaps even share an expression of Jesus' character with others without realizing it? No, it isn't crazy, because Jesus is the answer to all people's problems! Most everyone, Christian or not, knows people who are hurting and desires to give them something that will lift them up. Granted, the nonbeliever may not identify it with an articulation of the gospel, but Jesus still reveals himself through character traits that come from him. Couldn't Jesus reveal himself on someone's journey when they're seeking one or more of those very expressions? We know that the most encouraging word is the gospel lived out; it doesn't only meet people's personal needs but also meets their need to be equipped to help others.

It's critical to design a waypoint around an outcome because of the next, closely related test.

The Continuity Test

The continuity test asks, **"How well does this lead someone to commit to a new constant?"** The potentiality test and the continuity test go hand in hand because waypoints and constants go hand in hand to produce outcomes—or said another way, stations and trains go hand in hand to take people to destinations. So a waypoint passes the continuity test when it facilitates a next step into a constant (a consistent church engagement or a personal habit) that people are likely to take. It fails when it is not tied to an ongoing engagement, when the next step is a bigger stretch than people are likely to make, or when the practicalities of how to take that step are confusing.

Let's take the third outcome above: "How am I sharing the gospel with people who don't know Jesus?" Imagine designing a special event waypoint that would even inspire nonbelievers to learn more about the gospel so that they could share it with others. (I know it seems implausible—but stay with me.)

Imagine a waypoint called "Timeless Truths for the Cancer Journey: An Evening for Patients and Their Loved Ones." In this event, cancer survivors in your church and the people who cared for them share about what they learned that got them through. The survivors tell stories about how particular gospel principles shared by their loved ones were critical to give them the strength they needed. The supporters talk about how they learned to show empathy to their loved ones and give just the right word at just the right moment. Unbelievers wouldn't have to believe the gospel to be uplifted by the stories of people's journeys and be intrigued by the gospel principles they're hearing along the way.

But what's the next step? The continuity test requires the way-point to lead people into a constant (an ongoing activity or a personal habit) pointed in the same direction. In this example, the event could invite people into an ongoing training class and support group for people taking care of loved ones with cancer. Week after week that constant would combine practical wisdom with gospel truth to equip caregivers with good words to share with their loved ones. But at the same time, the discussions could also lead caregivers to eventually consider their own journey and potential relationship with Christ, the ultimate caregiver. At the end of the training class, participants could be given a personal invitation into long-term groups to grow on their journey toward (or in) Christ through ongoing relationships. That becomes another waypoint—another pivotal moment—because it would point them to the next constant or next train they could take as they make progress on their journey to God's destination for their lives.

Getting people to move from the waypoint to a next step requires leaders to explore thought-provoking, nitty-gritty questions. For example, during the waypoint, how does a person signal their interest in taking the next step? How do they ask questions to learn more about it? How do they get acquainted with the people who will lead it? How do they get comfortable with what it entails? How do they learn when and where it meets? How will they be reminded to come? How will they know what to bring or how to get what they need?

It is equally important to offer a decisive, concrete step both *in* the waypoint and *after* the waypoint. You want to get people to do something or say something—preferably face-to-face—that expresses their intention to engage the constant in some way for the

MIND THE GAP

first time. But some people will never do that in the first moment they're confronted with the option; they're wired in such a way that they have to think things over. So, you also need a plan to enable them to express that decisive intention after the waypoint ends.

Focused Quality Control Criteria for Constants

Now that we've looked at the three focused criteria specific to "Pepsi," the waypoints, we can look at the three for "Coke," the constants.

The Intentionality Test

We begin with the intentionality test, which asks, **"How well does this produce growth of desired outcomes in people's lives?"** A constant passes the intentionality test when participants grow in the church's defined journey outcomes because leaders have intentionally focused and structured the constant to cultivate those outcomes. It fails when ongoing engagement in the constant doesn't produce change in participants' lives.

We've already touched on this idea in the discussion of the potentiality test for waypoints to get people to focus on a *potential* outcome for their lives. The intentionality test for constants reveals how well we're creating conditions that actually produce growth in those outcomes. We've already seen that stations should be designed to get people onto trains, and trains should carry people to destinations. The one point to add is that most constants don't fit just one outcome. For example, a mid-sized teaching and training environment probably should help people progress toward multiple defined destinations of deepening growth in Christ. One quarter, one discipleship outcome (or several related outcomes) might be the focus of teaching, modeling, and practicing, and the next quarter, the focus might shift to a different outcome.

The intentionality test, then, requires ministry designers and front-line leaders to select their content and structure their process to encourage people toward the whole spectrum of journey outcomes over time. Senior leaders also need to keep tabs on the variety of outcome emphases currently happening across the church's ministries. It's so important to develop checkup loops between layers of leadership for this very reason, to know what aspects of growth in Christ are being highlighted, which are being overemphasized, and which are being neglected. Feedback and intentionality are even more critical when you want to focus the whole church system on the most important need or opportunity right now. (We'll look more closely at these concepts later.)

The Vitality Test

Closely related to the intentionality test is the vitality test. This test asks, **"How well does this maintain or increase participants' interest over time?"** A constant passes the vitality test when participants stay active in it because it's both steadily consistent and continually varied. It keeps a person's interest because it feels reliable while also staying fresh and relevant. It fails when it's led inconsistently or becomes stale.

Our natural tendency is to think that once we get something started, it will just keep running on its own. It's a bit like Isaac Newton's first law of motion: an object in motion will stay in motion unless acted on by an unbalanced force. If you leave Earth and go on a space walk and throw a ball, that ball will continue out into space in the direction and speed you threw it more or less forever.

But we all know from experience that you can't replicate that experiment on Earth, because everything

A thriving constant is both steady and varied.

here has unbalanced forces acting on it—gravity and friction. Everything that moves is pulled toward the center of the planet, and it has other matter—solid, liquid, or gas—grinding on it and slowing it down.

The same is true for the constants that we run in our churches and that individuals run in their lives. Even though establishing a routine greatly helps a constant keep moving forward, there is always gravity and friction exerting subtle pressure on it to slow down or stop. There are always distractions, difficulties, and even times of sheer boredom that can exert drag on the regular, reliable, consistent operations of the church.

Therefore, what's often overlooked is that it takes *proactive effort* to keep a constant going at the same rate (consider the second choir ministry described earlier). To keep a ministry thriving, deliberate oversight is required both by the leader of the constant and by the leader who holds that leader accountable.

Just as we tend to falsely assume that a constant will just keep going of its own accord, we also falsely assume that people will just keep participating of their own accord. It's easy to overlook the truth that winning someone to a constant is not a once and done thing. Even if they've been involved for months or even years, we never stop having to win them, because there are plenty of other things trying to win them away from that commitment.

The vitality test requires ministry designers and front-line leaders to keep things interesting, to add just the right amount of variety and novelty to regular activities to spice things up without offending the palate. Perhaps the most powerful feature of a constant that draws in newcomers is that it also keeps drawing in regulars, not because they're used to coming but because they're getting more from the engagement.

The vitality test also has huge implications for the personal habits we encourage in disciples' lives. Many leaders expend great effort to get people to start a daily habit of reading the Bible. But how much effort is given to *keeping* people growing in their *literacy* of the Bible? It's not for nothing that Bible reading and listening platforms create and host a range of diverse reading plans and studies to keep things interesting. We can actively encourage people not only to swap between plans but to swap between apps. We can sync up a campaign where the whole church is invited to read the same thing for three weeks. We can design studies that equip them to go deeper in their personal literacy and understanding of *how* to approach the Bible. The sky's the limit when it comes to variation. All of these can keep things from getting stale and give people chance after chance to not only get on the train, but at times to get *back* on it.

The Expectancy Test

The last focused test for constants is the expectancy test. It asks, **"How well is this designed with the participant's probable future in mind?"** A constant passes the expectancy test when it sets participants up well for the next logical step to take. It fails when a predictable change happens in the participant's life, and the constant is too inflexible to absorb the change or smoothly transition the person to the next step.

The most glaring place to apply this test is age-graded constants. Every children's ministry leader knows that their children will become teenage students. Every student ministry leader knows their students will become young adults. The pattern continues long into adulthood. Wise leaders apply the expectancy test to design ministry so that it not only shepherds people toward destinations where they are but also prepares them for how their discipleship journey will change as they move to the next life stage.

The expectancy test applies to other examples as well. If a married woman begins regularly attending a constant without her husband, we as leaders should design that constant *expecting* that at some point she'd like to invite him to join her at church. Is the constant prepared for that? Is it designed to accommodate him and pass the empathy test whatever his "point A" may be? I've seen many well-intended churches let women's (or men's) ministries become such a church within a church, that they end up becoming a relational barrier to the other partner being able to join his or her spouse in the future. The first spouse becomes so close to and so involved in the single-gender ministry (vs. connected multiple-gender opportunities), that the other spouse will always be excluded. The issue is not whether to have vibrant men's and women's ministries; it's designing them with clear *connectivity* to fit potential outcomes based on people's journeys downstream.

In a way, the expectancy test is the echo of all the other tests. Ministry designers always need to ask the question "what's next?" *What is this ministry aiming for? Where are people going? What will they need next? How do we meet them there?*

Criteria for constants and waypoints	The empathy test	How well does this show appreciation for where people are when they first engage?
	The proximity test	How well does your space and intimacy design match with participants' willingness to get close?
	The totality test	How well does this both expand the mind and move the heart?
	The variability test	How well do we vary the intensity and type of communicated emotion in this?
	The spirituality test	How well does this disciple people spiritually as they serve?
Focused criteria for waypoints	The curiosity test	How well does this grab people's attention so that they want to know more?
	The potentiality test	How well does this focus people's attention on a potential outcome for their life?
	The continuity test	How well does this lead someone to commit to a new constant?

Focused criteria for constants	The intentionality test	How well does this produce growth of desired outcomes in people's lives?
	The vitality test	How well does this maintain or increase participants' interest over time?
	The expectancy test	How well is this designed with the participant's probable future in mind?

Table 2: Quality Control Criteria for Constants and Waypoints

This is the kind of intentional forward thinking that marks a shepherd, a farmer, and a builder. This is the kind of system sensitivity that cares about how each ministry engagement cooperates with all the others to offer the right "next moves" to a broad diversity of people on their individual journeys with God.

Designing such a system is absolutely critical, but even the most perfect system doesn't make disciples. Only disciples do through the power of God's Spirit as they engage with others. So, in order **for people to move forward toward God's destinations, they need stations and trains, but they also need traveling companions** along the way. The next chapter is about how to breathe life into the integrated ministry system by teaming up with metapartners in close-contact disciple-making.

{ CHAPTER 9 }

Traveling Companions: How Metapartners Help People Make Their Next Move

On the first page of this book, I mentioned that I'm an organizational consultant who spends a lot of time with ministry leaders. But without filling in the details, that could mean just about anything. So I'd like to tell you more of my story here, because it illuminates how to move your ministry beyond a drawing board system on paper to a living system in people.

My professional career didn't start in the church but in higher education administration, years before my ordination as a minister. I served in various executive roles, teaching, conducting research, and facilitating strategic growth and fundraising initiatives at different institutions ranging from large, tier-one research universities to a major medical school to private Christian universities. In serving a variety of campaigns raising more than a billion dollars over the years, I've worked closely with a wide range of people—from students, faculty, and staff, to donors, alumni, volunteers, congregation members, and church and community leaders—to figure out how they tick and create meaningful ways to deepen their personal engagement and investment in the vision. God called me to broaden the application of these principles through leadership roles at national and global ministries, on a large church staff, and ultimately a wide-reaching consulting ministry. I've been described not only as a culture and leadership coach but also as a pastor to pastors.

Learning why people's connection to certain things grows and their connection to others doesn't has been a fascination of mine all the way along. During my PhD work, I explored how principles of strategic process improvement can help leaders pinpoint the few, most critical areas to focus on in their unique context to maximize the engagement and effectiveness of others. This is all the more crucial in the fast-changing, increasingly complex world we live in. With the overwhelming amount of information and options leaders have access to daily, it's more important than ever for them to filter the noise to mind what really matters.

Intriguingly and a bit surprisingly, I discovered through personal experience as a church leader that the best lessons I'd learned on engaging people in philanthropy helped stimulate discipleship growth *that had nothing to do with raising money*. I found that whether I was working with investors entrusting their wealth to an organization or with disciples entrusting their lives to God, I was attempting to facilitate much of the same thing—to progressively deepen their attention on and engagement with a greater vision that transforms themselves and others. Once I realized that from the university to the church, I always had been in the business of deepening people's heart commitment to a mission, disciple-making lessons bubbled up everywhere.

Making Disciples by Making the Right Next Move

Let me illustrate by taking you behind the curtain of professional philanthropic advancement for a moment. Across the spectrum of not-for-profit organizations, you'll find a variety of fundraising approaches that leaders use based on their vision, context, and perspective on what works. Two such approaches are at different ends of the spectrum. The first is focused on short-term efficiency; it involves soliciting donations by trying to get the most contributions possible at the present time with the lowest overhead costs. An example you're familiar with might be a mass appeal or digital campaign to get as many people as possible to donate relatively small amounts to a particular cause. As fundraising strategies go, these don't cost much, because for the reach of the appeal, they don't require many people-hours to pull them off.

At the other end of the spectrum, a second approach is focused on long-term effectiveness. This approach involves cultivating genuine relationships with prospective or current donors to determine what their needs are and, based on those needs, to go on a journey together that leads their engagement and commitment deeper. It is far more resource-intensive, largely because it requires a lot more time and intentionality. But when done right, it pays off in the long run in the form of much larger gifts, sometimes truly transformational ones, because the donors see themselves as personally investing in a mission that matters to them deeply.

In the philanthropic realm, the teams I've led have been entrusted with a circle of prospective donors who were considered strong prospects to support the organization's mission at a high level. These were people who already had both substantial wealth and significant interest (or potential interest) in what the organization was doing to transform lives. Our job was to invite them into the story to engage them in ways that might deepen their passion for and investment in the vision.

Each of these potential investment partners had an unconscious mental box—what I call a "connection box"—where they placed the organization. The size of this box in their minds represented their personal conviction and the amount they might be inclined to invest based on their current perceptions about the organization's calling and results. I was essentially building genuine relationships that inspired their connection box to grow over time both in mind and heart—helping them develop and accomplish what was consistent with their needs and interests through opportunities the organization was providing. Along the way, I sought to deepen their personal passion, in-person involvement, and desire to engage others, so the person would become a partner to reach even more people.

So how does an effective philanthropic professional go about cultivating that kind of relationship? It doesn't come from short-term mass appeals or digital campaigns. No one's connection box expands to five, six, seven, eight, or more digits because each month they get two emails or letters from an organization instead of one. It also doesn't expand by someone calling around dinner time and asking for 1.7 million dollars.

What's crucial to remember in cultivating such a relationship is that it's a *relationship*. Relationships get deeper by degrees. They don't come about impersonally, nor do they often develop suddenly. It requires becoming a genuine part of the person's life with meaningful frequency and continuity. It requires understanding where the person is, so to speak—what they are thinking and feeling, what their life is like, what they care about, what they wonder about, what excites their interest, who they interact with and who means something to them. Along the way, the leader carefully personalizes and offers a progressive series of relational next moves— with each next move being a reasonable, attractive, actionable step that fosters greater involvement. This sophisticated discipline of cultivating a person's deeper engagement based on their unique wiring is called moves management.[1]

Over time, the plan is to escort the person over many smaller moves to greater awareness, then to understanding, then ultimately to appreciation and passion for a much bigger, life-changing vision the organization can help meet. Some moves on these journeys involve asking the person for a gift; most of them don't (until the time is right). But the whole immersive journey depends on thoughtfully designing the next right move that fosters growth, time after time after time, based on the person's interaction during the prior move.

---

1. Now a staple of the major gifts profession, moves management was pioneered by David Dunlop and G. T. "Buck" Smith, and advanced through organizations such as the Institute for Charitable Giving under the leadership of the legendary Jerry Panas and William T. Sturtevant. The term *Moves Management* is registered by the Institute for Charitable Giving.

From a development perspective, when considering the next move with a person, the focus is on fostering interaction points that would be most meaningful for them on their journey of growing interest in the vision. That could include planning "primary activities" like a one-on-one meeting with a key leader whose name came up in conversation or a planned group event to dialogue with other major supporters on a thought-provoking topic connected to the vision. Sometimes it might be a role serving on a team together to experience a vision's impact firsthand or partnering with others to explore creative or challenging ways to expand the reach of the vision. There also would be supportive "background activities," such as a personal note or enjoying a hobby together or an invitation to a social gathering to spend time with others whose lives had been changed through their involvement with the vision. Sometimes it involved providing genuine support to the person in other unrelated areas of his or her life as needs came up.

The possibilities of how to set these up are nearly endless and depend very much on the unique context and calling of both the organization and individual. To give a few specific examples, in a university or medical school setting, it might be a series exploring innovative partnerships with community leaders, an event celebrating life-changing student accomplishments, dinner with a prominent faculty researcher, or a personal tour through a new laboratory for cancer research. In ministries or churches it might include creative ways to see the ministry's impact on certain people groups, immersive experiences to enrich one's own marriage while learning about ways to reach countless others, or meetings with potential ministry partners to dream about what could leverage greater kingdom impact.

Whatever it is, however, the contact by itself is not a move. What makes it a move is the intentionality that goes into it that leads to something more and helps the person uncover that *they want* something more. It's a thoughtfully arranged, natural next step that puts the person first and progressively helps increase their knowledge of, interest in, or commitment to the vision while on a relational journey with others.

You may be starting to see some intriguing overlap to goals of disciple-making. The process of guiding a person to a place of transformational sacrifice in giving of themselves and their money reveals discipleship lessons we can learn from. The relevance shouldn't surprise us. With over two thousand Bible verses on the topic, we should be especially attuned to what works in cultivating this kind of growth and passion. The system design that nurtures overflowing generosity reveals much about how God has created people to process and grow, both mind and heart. Indeed, the moves-process *is* a deep discipling of people toward something more that's stirring both in them and beyond them—reflecting powerful principles of how God has wired people to move toward something greater, through the prompting of his Spirit, that he has for their lives.

We can think of these principles as *five layers of disciple-moving*. They stack on top of each other and all work together; you can't consistently help the breadth of your people take their next moves with Christ unless all five layers are active and integrated into your system. The first three of the five layers take key ideas we've already explored in this book and summarize them in light of moves management. The fourth layer introduces an important new principle. We'll discuss all four of these layers in this chapter, then look at the fifth layer in the next.

THE FIVE LAYERS OF DISCIPLE-MOVING

1. Lead deeply
2. Know fully
3. Arrange wisely
4. Partner informatively
5. Learn repeatedly

Lead Deeply

First, moves management and disciple-making both need to proactively lead people to **ever deeper engagement and commitment**. In philanthropy, the process seeks to inspire people to deep identification with and personal sacrifice for an organization. In ministry, as followers of Jesus obeying his Great Commission, the process should help bring a person to such a deep identification with Christ that they would give their entire being to him.

Just as a philanthropic professional would never intend for an investor's first gift to an organization to be their last, it's the same with a person's commitment to follow Christ. Without a doubt, when a person crosses the line of faith to accept Jesus as Lord, they experience a new birth, a transfer from death to life. But the initial commitment is just the beginning. To each of his followers, Jesus keeps revealing more, directing more, calling us deeper, stretching us further toward conformity to his image and living out the purpose he made us for.

> Jesus reveals more as we respond to his call to lead more deeply.

Given this, for leaders to create systems that stretch and multiply disciple-making disciples throughout their entire church means they must be committed to leading more deeply than they ever imagined. They must see themselves as God's agents to create a collective relational framework—based on their church's unique missional calling—that helps more and more people recognize and say yes to the bigger and bigger "asks" God lays on their life as they deepen their personal identification with him. This requires leaders' obsessive attention to improvement in how their systems are designed to move all of their people—both collectively and individually—ever deeper into spiritual outcomes on their journeys.

Expecting anything less of ourselves as leaders is shallow and shortsighted.

Know Fully

Second, moves management and disciple-making both need to **know a person genuinely and conscientiously**. This includes having a keen understanding about where they are on their journey, as well as what they seek and what they need.

Effective philanthropic professionals do significant research on those in their circle and then learn more as they build genuine relationships with them. They want to know where they've lived, where they've worked, why they've been successful, what their hobbies are, what other causes they've supported and why, what their beliefs are, what community, public, or military service they've performed, what motivates them, even what the most emotionally significant events in their life have been. As genuine relationships grow, they get personal.

The intent is to get to know each person well enough to understand their needs and inspire and partner with them to explore
· ways investment opportunities might help fulfill the impact they
long for in the world. In doing so, I've actually had multiple seven-
figure donors thank me for the opportunity to give! At that point,
it wasn't just a contribution to them; it was a significant step on
their life journey.

In reading the New Testament, I'm struck by how much care
Jesus and the apostles took to know where people were spiritually,
emotionally, and every other way, and how carefully they engaged
people at that place. Jesus knew the woman at the well was thirsty
in more ways than one, so he offered her living water. He knew the
crowds on the desolate shore were hungry, so he called himself the
bread of life. Philip knew that the eunuch of Ethiopia was examining the prophecies of Isaiah, so he asked him if he could understand
it. Peter knew that Cornelius had spent years worshipping the God
of Israel from a distance as an unclean Gentile, so he spoke of how
God shows no favoritism. Paul knew that the Athenians were afraid
of failing to appease an unknown god, so he introduced the God
they did not know in terms amenable to Stoic philosophy. Time
and again, the first disciple-makers of our faith took keen interest
in knowing as much as they could about the people they sought to
bring into deeper engagement with the kingdom, and they made
the most of what they knew.

As a reminder, this is why outcomes-based tools like Mind the
Gap Surveys are so important. It certainly doesn't take the place
of knowing people well who you're personally leading into deeper
commitments with Christ. That's every leader's (and every disciple's) responsibility. Still, as leaders, we only can know so many

people that well, and can personally invest in even fewer than that. Meanwhile, we have a whole church to shepherd. We must create purposeful tools that provide touchpoints in a system to know where all of our people are on their journeys toward the destinations God has for them. (I'll share another tool shortly—the checkup loop—that will help you with this.) As leaders, we must pursue this "widespread knowing" as fully as possible to understand what's working and what's not, and to be able to design next moves that truly engage all the people we're called to shepherd.

Arrange Wisely

That leads us to the third parallel between moves management and disciple-making: both need to have a **rhythm of determining the best next moves** that will take people to deeper engagement. Remember, these moves should be clear and defined based on their interaction in and response to prior moves.

As we discussed how to cultivate deeper relationships between people and organizations based on the individual's needs, I bet you saw parallels to disciple-making. That intentional posture is especially relevant given the eternal significance of cultivating a deeper relationship between a disciple and Jesus and his calling for their lives. As a disciple maker, you know how important it is to discern how the Spirit is prompting you to be part of a disciple's next move. Everyone has a next step to take on their journey with Christ, whether that's installing a godly habit, breaking an ungodly one, engaging with a group of people, pursuing knowledge, or serving someone, somewhere. Inviting a disciple to a next step that doesn't align with *both* their next need *and* their current conception of what they need just doesn't work. The person won't take it, or if they do just to appease us, they often quietly drift away later.

We know by experience that this is what happens, but how often do church leaders still approach the largest majority of their people thoughtlessly? It's painfully common for leaders not to take a person's present spiritual condition as a given to accommodate themselves to, but instead to take their church's ministry structure as the given to force the person into. (Many don't realize they're doing this because they don't truly *know* the person's present condition as described earlier.) When this happens, instead of inviting a person into the next move that's right for them, we invite them into what's right for us because it's easier to manage or it makes the numbers in a ministry area look good. For example, referencing a story from an earlier chapter, you might recall how familiar it is for some leaders to tell everyone in a church to get in a group, any group, as if that's the cure-all prescription. Though group participation may be important, that may not be everyone's most important *next* move. And even if someone's next move *is* to get in a group, it probably isn't to get into just *any* group offered. They will likely need a specific kind of group with a specific slant. But all that nuance is lost when we don't have an interconnected system with defined ways to determine and invite people to the right next move.

Let me be clear: I'm not advocating for a consumeristic posture willing to give anything to buy anyone's attention and then hoping that things just work out. For sure, when you only care about what people want and not what they need, you don't lead anyone anywhere. But if you only care about what people need and not what they *think* they want, you almost always set up a next move that's too far for them to leap to, and then you lose credibility to lead them anywhere. Knowing and caring about what people currently want is essential to wisely arranging the right waypoints and constants to get them to what they ultimately need.

Naturally, it's much easier to invite someone into the right next move if you know them well. But once again, we're limited by how many people in our church we can know deeply, whether because of the constraints of time and relational bandwidth or because people hesitate to reveal face-to-face what is really going on in their lives. Remember, an outcomes-based approach to evalu-

> Be mindful of what people *need* as well as what they *think* they need.

ation gives you a view of the entirety of your church. If journey-focused surveys and checkup loops (which I'll describe in detail shortly) are presented well, people are refreshingly honest in their responses. It serves as a much more useful basis for discerning *the way you're going to design and arrange* the right next moves for the most people instead of making churchwide decisions based on a few stories here and there. With a view of the whole, you're able to see what outcomes aren't being developed in people's lives. Better yet, when you drill down into different demographic segments, you're able to identify more specific areas of need and tailor solutions to the people who need them most.

Those solutions come in the form of your church's waypoints and constants—its stations and trains—that lead to outcomes in people's lives on their journey (destinations). The next moves you set up for people are designed as a chain from waypoint to constant to waypoint to constant, a multistage path through the church Underground leading to destinations. Having an integrated ministry system like this is enormously helpful when you're helping someone take their next move, because you have relevant, concrete steps to invite people to take. A nimbly responsive, thoughtfully designed system gives them the right options for the most pressing needs of the most people right now. When people are offered more fitting next steps, the percentage of people who actually take them increases tremendously.

Partner Informatively

The first three parallels between moves management and disciple-making connect to areas we've already looked at closely in earlier chapters on outcomes, constants, and waypoints. The fourth layer of disciple moving, on the other hand, we've only briefly mentioned to this point. I summarize it this way: both moves management and disciple-making **need to work with others** who are close to the organization's mission and close to the people you're engaging. In moves management, these allies are commonly called natural partners.[2] This idea is even more important to biblical disciple-making in a church than it is to cultivating major gifts. In a moment, I'll introduce a new term and definition for ministry contexts, and describe how strategically involving laypeople as on-the-ground partners makes a ministry system come alive.

Remember, in advancing philanthropy, it's helpful to learn everything possible about a potential investor. A crucial element of this is the web of relationships around the person. In building relationships, we would discover the identities of their colleagues,

---

2. William T. Sturtevant, *The Artful Journey: Cultivating and Soliciting the Major Gift* (Chicago: Institutions Press, 2004).

financial advisors, attorneys, and yes, pastors. We were interested in learning about friends and family members who already were enthusiastic supporters of the organization.

Any of these people around the prospective donor could become our partners, depending on the stages and steps of the relationship building process. Like a team coach, serving as a "moves manager" means identifying and managing people with the best skill, experience, and relationship, and matching them up at the right time with the right message and right goal. These partners are people who already have bought into the vision and have made significant personal sacrifice for its success. They are passionate about what the organization is trying to achieve. Given their relationship with the person, they can help think through what kinds of contacts, approaches, or strategies might work best in certain situations. As we worked and planned moves together, they would leverage their access to the prospective donor in natural settings to ease relational development, open doors to new people or new ideas, provide testimonials, and/or even serve as solicitation partners when it made sense.

Requests of the partner would be specific, measurable, and time-bound. The partner would be prepared to share key parts of the vision, and also have specific options for a reasonable next step based on the progression of the discussion. Afterward, we would follow up with the partner, learn more about the donor, and together we would use that information to design next moves suited to the donor's needs and what they cared about most. (Note that our involvement of the partner also constituted a next move to further strengthen that person's passion as well.)

When I take people behind the scenes of not-for-profit fund-raising as I'm doing here, sometimes they feel a bit uncomfortable, thinking it might be manipulative. However, at its core, moves management is all about building authentic relationships that, when done correctly, are in the best interests of everyone at a far deeper level. A philanthropic guide is someone who gets to know and be known by donors up close. An ethical development professional doesn't portray their organization or themselves as something they aren't or put the organization's interest above the donor. Rather, the whole enterprise is based on something worthwhile that everyone—moves managers, natural partners, and donors alike—transparently share in common: they all genuinely love the organization's vision and want to engage others in it to experience the joy of transformational impact.

Like moves management, disciple-making also is all about authentic relationships built around things that everyone in that relationship cares about. Whenever you find something you love, you naturally want to share it with others and spend time with them talking about it. "The world rings with praise," C. S. Lewis writes.[3] How true this is when our lives have been changed by Christ! If you know him, you want others to know him. If you experienced his power to set you free from addiction, for example, you're especially attuned to others with addictions because you want every addicted person to experience it too. And if you're an addicted person considering getting help, you're glad for a friend who understands and believes in what they're talking about to walk with you along the way. Regardless of the circumstance,

---

3. C. S. Lewis, *Reflections on the Psalms* (New York: Harcourt, Brace and World, 1958), 93.

God's plan becomes more clear when his people become more and more sensitive to his calling in their lives to reach others wherever they are on their journey.

In the church, that's really what this kind of partner can be: a traveling companion on the journey through a church's stations and trains toward the destinations God has for their lives. They aren't working behind the counter of an information booth, telling people where to go but not going there themselves. They too are on the journey to the same destinations, the same journey outcomes, because they passionately believe in them. They've probably just been doing it in the church a bit longer or have a special clarity for the importance of coming alongside others. They've personally experienced or learned the value of the trains and stations and know well what the church Underground has to offer. They want to help others take the journey with them and want to help others make their next move.

Unleash Your Lay Leader Impact through Metapartnering

Within a ministry context, I want to propose a different term for the approach I just described: *metapartnering*. Miriam-Webster defines "meta" as "showing or suggesting an explicit awareness of itself or oneself" or as in the case of the term *meta*physics "more comprehensive: transcending."[4] My use of this intends to communicate a more comprehensive commitment to the idea of partnering with lay leaders in our churches in a deeply aware way. This type of

---

4. *Merriam Webster*, s.v. "meta," https://www.merriam-webster.com/dictionary/meta.

overarching attention and connectedness is consistent with the way many church leaders examine the *meta*narrative of Scripture. I also like the connection to the transformational idea of *meta*morphosis, both to transform our thinking about lay partners and to remind us of the new life in Christ that people will experience as a result.

There are three required attributes for metapartners that you as a leader should seek out and nurture. I call them the Three Cs of Metapartners: Close, Curious, and Collaborative. First, metapartners must be *close*. They must be close to you and the church's mission and also to the people you are trying to reach. They need to have close natural and consistent "on-the-ground" connections with other people in the church. Second, they must be *curious*. Metapartners shouldn't simply be good volunteers or implementers; you want them to have a mindset of experimentation and insatiable curiosity to help you find out where people really are and why certain things may or may not be working as well as they could to help them grow in your church's outcomes. And third, metapartners must be Collaborative. You're not looking for lone rangers to get an assignment done on their own. You want people who desire to collaborate with you and the other metapartners you work with to compare ideas, synthesize findings, and help you discern new ways to continually improve your church's disciple-making system.

THE THREE Cs OF METAPARTNERS

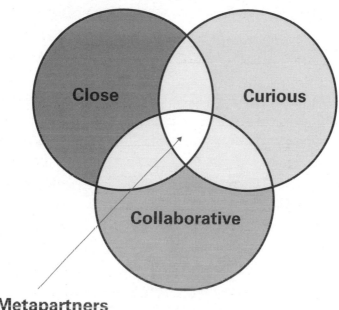

Metapartners

The goal is for each of your key staff leaders to have a group of metapartners to train and work with consistently (I'll explain the process in a moment). Anyone in your church can be a metapartner, because every disciple is authorized in (and called to!) the Great Commission to make other disciples—to help people take their next step with Christ. However, as a ministry "moves manager" seeking to design an integrated system, it's most useful to identify and develop metapartners as focused groups of on-the-ground frontline lay leaders who each key staff leader is working with.

Often, these will be lay leaders who are leading defined ministry teams or small to mid-sized groups, whether in the whole church or in the particular area of ministry you or other staff leaders oversee. Lay leaders of constants and lay leaders of waypoints can both be metapartners, even though a constant leader's relationship with people is ongoing while a waypoint leader's may be significantly shorter, sometimes even just a few minutes long.

Now, as I counsel you to focus on frontline leaders as good potential metapartners, I am *not* saying that they're automatically metapartners as we're defining them. Remember, metapartners are invested in the organization's mission, vision, and expectations as articulated by your desired outcomes and outcome expressions. Said a different way, being invested means they're passionately committed to shepherding people in your church's specific definition of success. They're also *connected to and trained by their ministry moves manager in specific roles as part of an ongoing two-way feedback process called a checkup loop,* which I'll describe to you shortly. This will give you what you need to plan, launch, evaluate, and improve ministry approaches nimbly as you go.

It's critical not to assume any of this from your leaders just because they're currently leading. Drawing them into the kind of personal commitment to the vision and expectation as metapartners to guide others to that same commitment isn't a given, and developing it doesn't happen all at once. The good news is that the process of involving metapartners that I'm about to describe might be the very thing that turns decent frontline leaders into sold-out mission evangelists.

Yes, in disciple-making ministry, metapartners can give you a consistent, two-way bridge of communication that frees you to achieve a whole new level of effectiveness. The metapartner forms a checkup loop with a ministry moves manager, helping that senior leader get remarkable insight and a much clearer view of what's happening in people's lives *in real time*—such as how specific ministry initiatives or experiments are working or not in growing clearly understood journey outcomes, and what the true barriers are to people realizing that deeper growth. On the other side, by helping to navigate the church participant's journey as a fellow traveler, the metapartner is able to proactively present and encourage the best possible options for people's next moves toward destinations of transformation.

This gift of ongoing insight for leaders is an invaluable part of the fifth layer—to **learn repeatedly**. A lifestyle of continually learning more so we can impact more bears fruit beyond imagination. I will discuss this fifth layer more in the next chapter.

Introducing the Checkup Loop: Your Engine for the Five Layers

When church leaders look for insight, they often tend to go to leaders outside their church. They might go to a conference, buy a book, subscribe to a podcast, or talk with colleagues in other churches.

Of course external sources of information can be helpful to a leader; if I didn't think so, I wouldn't be writing this book. The problem arises when leaders try to borrow or copy ministry *program* approaches that are successful elsewhere and assume those "solutions" also will work in their unique context—which they rarely do to the same degree if at all. Copying specific programs or program approaches often feels like a shot in the dark or a game

of Whack-a-Mole. This is vastly different from focusing on growing your leadership acumen—the way you think, assess, and make
decisions—to better design, evaluate, and improve your system in
ongoing ways.

To do this, church leaders must face a big problem I see all the
time: neglecting deeper insight from the best source of evaluative
knowledge about their ministry context—the frontline lay leaders
in their own church. If properly trained and mobilized using the
kind of integrated system we're discussing, these people are a gold
mine. They may not yet have insight about the big picture, but they
have a wealth of insight about their small pictures, which is where
senior leaders' big-picture plans often flounder.

Most of us agree with this in principle and are even pretty confident that we appreciate the input of our leaders. But I don't think
we seek it and embrace it as much as we think we do. I'm talking
about something much deeper.

Let's face it: on one end of the communication spectrum, there
are pastors who rarely communicate with their leaders just like they
rarely communicate with their washer and dryer. Once a leader has
been acquired and installed as a volunteer, they're tacitly expected
to keep quietly doing their thing. Other than an occasional voice
of appreciation or brief celebration, they aren't noticed until something breaks or they're suddenly gone.

Many more pastors, I think, take time talking with their leaders,
but they don't learn all that much from the conversation. This often
is because many pastors live in *get-it-done* mode. They're focused on
the next event or initiative or rollout, and they're just trying to relay
the necessary information to pull it off. The only feedback they're

expecting from leaders is probably a few questions to clarify something or confirm that they know what they're supposed to do.

Other pastors spend time in encouragement mode with their leaders. They care about their lives, ask them how they're doing, even shepherd them spiritually. They might hear a good deal of what the person is thinking and feeling, but it's mostly about the leader's experience, not much about anyone or anything else except for a few points here and there. Pastors engage in these personal conversations because they genuinely care, but also hope to keep the leaders feeling good enough about serving that they'll keep doing it.

Some pastors engage with their leaders in coaching mode, which is more substantial. They have regular conversations with their leaders to develop their competency and character and discuss how those relate to projects or ministries of the church. Through conversations like these, pastors may hear a lot more about what's really going on in ministry environments. But because the main focus of these conversations is the leader's development, not what's happening in the lives of people the leader serves, deeper valuable feedback may not surface or be retained consistently.

Getting things done, encouraging, and coaching all are necessary when leading leaders. But none of them is a substitute for the checkup loop. The checkup loop is an exchange of views for the specific purpose of giving a ministry moves manager what he or she needs to lead responsively—a true, deep understanding of what's happening on the front lines in real time.

A working checkup loop in a church setting follows a five-step cycle:

THE CHECKUP LOOP

1
FOCUS
Prepare your
metapartners
on a topic

2
SEND
Dispatch your
metapartners
to research

3
SYNTHESIZE
Capture
themes from
the data

4
ACT
Use your findings
to execute
a next step

5
EVALUATE
Assess results
to plan your
next move

Step 1: FOCUS: Prepare Your Metapartners on a Topic

The checkup loop first becomes relevant when you administer a congregational outcomes survey, as described in chapter 3. Remember, you've already established your core groups of metapartners who are committed to seeing your church's outcomes realized in people's lives. And the details of those outcomes (outcome expressions) are measured one by one in that survey to give you *baseline* awareness of where your people are in all of them. The survey results give you a wealth of critical information you wouldn't have otherwise, but that's only a starting point. It's critical to then explore the survey results with your metapartners, get their initial thoughts, and then mobilize them to find out *why* people responded they way they did and how the results seem to manifest themselves in the lives of people they're in touch with. The preparation of your partners to have these conversations is Step 1 of the checkup loop.

For example, let's say you find that a majority of people in the church (or certain segments of the church) are struggling to share the gospel. For one outcome expression after another, a majority said that the statement often was not true of them. The least-agreed-upon statement was "I frequently engage in spiritual conversations with people who are different from me or don't yet know Jesus."

To some degree, your frontline leaders probably already know that things aren't going well with this journey outcome. Some of them are among those who are struggling! Certainly the people they lead are. So first, your metapartners themselves become your focus group. Each ministry moves manager should lead a meeting with all the metapartners from their ministry area to discuss the outcome expressions on the survey you initially want to focus on. For example, in this case you could ask things like:

Why, in our unique context and community, do you think people responded this way?

What barriers do you think the people in your group might be facing to have spiritual conversations with people who don't know Jesus yet?

What can we supply you with that would make it easier to have honest conversations about this and help those in your group overcome their barriers?

What are some creative ways we can talk about this with our people to help them share honestly and stir their imagination? (As you engage this question, you'll plan and write a script of discussion bullets together so your leaders will be prepared for Step 2.)

Important: In this dialogue, you're not seeking right and wrong "religious" answers to questions. Instead, you're choosing thought-provoking angles to stoke curiosity among your leaders regarding *the true why* behind the survey responses. After a lively conversation around questions like these, you may end up with a list of what I call the *wandering maybes*—maybe it's this, maybe it's that, but you really don't know yet. This is a good place to be because hopefully it's stimulated your lay leaders' desire to find out the true why from their people.

By the end of this session, every lay leader should feel well prepared to be able to dialogue with their respective groups because you've landed on that approach and script together. Getting everyone on the same page about what they're going to ask is important because it ensures that everyone understands what they're looking for. Make sure they know what your specific expectations are on what to cover, when to cover it by, and what to report back on.

Step 2: SEND: Dispatch Your Metapartners to Research

Now that you've talked with your metapartners to pique their curiosity about certain survey data and to prep them for their research, it's time to send them out to discover the true why behind the data.

Metapartners should allow a good amount of time for the topic in an upcoming gathering that each group or team already has scheduled. For maximum engagement, they should ideally fit the discussion into their normal rhythm of meeting, not call a special meeting (though sometimes that's unavoidable). Someone other than the facilitator should take detailed anonymous notes. Remember, in Step 1, you would have already coached your metapartners on how to introduce the topic in positive ways so it doesn't come across as a form of admonishment or generate "expected" religious answers. Many people haven't even thought about the true whys behind their reticence or struggles, so give your partners piercing questions to help them peel the onion.

Some might be more naturally gifted at facilitating conversations like these than others, so a good practice is to have some of them share ideas or even model approaches in your Step 1 meeting. (Role plays can be fun and helpful if you've rehearsed them ahead of time!) Provide your leaders with three or four initial questions to ask their groups. For example, for the targeted topic above, you might use versions of the questions from Step 1, and/or others such as:

> What makes it hard to have spiritual conversations with others who don't know Jesus yet? What might make it feel more natural?

> Complete this sentence: "I would have more spiritual conversations with people who don't follow Jesus if I had . . ."

> Think about these three things for you personally: willingness to have a spiritual conversation, opportunity to have a spiritual conversation, ability to have a spiritual conversation. Give each one of these a personal rating from one to three, with one being "low" and three being "high." Ask everyone to share what they put and why.

> To help with your spiritual conversations, what's the best thing you can imagine inviting nonbelievers to, even if you or we have never done it? (no matter how small or big, whether church facilitated or something else)

For certain, the conversation begins with questions structured like these; it doesn't end with them. Your leaders need to become good facilitators of dialogue who learn how to ask follow-up questions to draw out of people's depths. With practice and encouragement this will become more and more natural. Still, having a focused start yields much better information than a vague, open-ended "what do you think?"

Step 3: SYNTHESIZE: Capture Themes from the Data

At this point, your leaders are beginning to function as genuine metapartners and field researchers. With their help, you'll learn a range of information about what's really happening, from confirmation of some things you might have suspected to other things that will blow your mind. You're going to learn what people are really doing (and not doing) and what they're honestly facing—their thoughts, feelings, fears, and exhilarations.

Breakthrough learning comes when you bring your metapartners back together and have a conversation on the specifics they found. As you review everyone's findings, capture and note the recurring themes you see. As a group, work to piece together the complex picture of what is happening and why. Identify and synthesize what appear to be the most influential factors without over-simplifying the data. Substantive conversations like these are where you'll finally, significantly start closing your *ongoing* awareness gaps.

By the way, I recommend meeting with your metapartners on a regular basis (six plus times per year) to share ongoing learnings, feedback, and best practices with one another as they emerge. Other planning topics for the ministry area can and should be covered in the same meeting, but a significant and consistent agenda item should be devoted to keeping the checkup loop turning. Remember, we're not talking about minding the gap as a one-time project; we're talking about it as an ongoing, ever-deepening culture.

Step 4: ACT: Use Your Findings to Execute a Next Step

Once you've closed the awareness gap by capturing what your metapartners learned, you're in a much better position to plan a good next step. If you've been reading the book up to this point instead of jumping straight to this chapter, you know that your next step is more than preaching a sermon series on the issue. It's time to close the connectivity gap. This is where your leadership team can carefully design a next move to be the right one for the right people.

This means examining your constants and waypoints and asking questions like these:

- Which organized activities (group constants) did we expect to produce this outcome in people's lives? Which personal habits (individual constants) did we expect to produce the outcome?
- To better shepherd growth in this key area we found, should we retool current constants, revise expectations, or create something new?
- How can we better equip or train our lay leaders based on what we now know?
- Of the people who are excelling in this outcome, do they have engagement in some constant in common?
- What is our success rate with getting people into the constants that would help them grow in this outcome?

- When was the last time we planned a waypoint specifically focused on this? How did it do at ramping people into the constants?
- Given the field research, what new waypoints do we need to create or which existing ones could we redesign?
- Based on where most people are today, what is a reachable next move that would stretch people just enough?

As you dialogue as a leadership team, you'll emerge with a clear plan to improve things or introduce something new, because you're basing it on clear data. But as you do this, don't forget the people you're doing it for—not only for the people in the church generally but also for your metapartners. Remember, these are your frontline leaders who are giving their time and resources to the Lord to serve his kingdom by serving your church. They aren't just marking time; they want to succeed. They want to see lives changed. The experiment you work up should have as its goal to help your metapartners get wins leading people to their next step with Christ. When they see you're making strong decisions on what they worked hard to uncover, their commitment will be deepened even more.

> Your metapartners should see clear decisions emerge from what they worked hard to uncover.

You help your metapartners succeed by giving them what they need to more effectively escort their people deeper into your church's journey outcomes. For example, you might implement improvements to a ministry area that will help focus people on the specific journey outcome or outcome expression you've been investigating. Let's say you're looking at something like this for your groups ministry. You could say:

> "You know how we've been talking about how our people aren't living out their good intentions to have spiritual conversations with their unbelieving friends? Well, we've designed a resource for group leaders on how to help their people deconstruct the seven main hesitancies they've shared with us. We're also planning a training event for leaders. Not only will it support them in the spiritual conversations they want to have based on our unique vision here at ABC Church, but it also will show them ways to walk their group through the same resource and incorporate it into their group's life together. Our goal is for all our group leaders to be able to celebrate seeing their people make real progress in this area. We'll share stories of growth and continue refining resources with one another in our regular monthly meetings together."

Based on the specific feedback you received on your people's challenges, you also might redefine the win for *waypoint* leaders to better fit your missional context. For example, let's say a church historically has held an annual community outreach event where they bring in a big speaker and encourage people to invite their nonbelieving friends. Church leaders might say the following:

> "This year we're going to try something different based on the specific challenges we've uncovered

about our people engaging in regular spiritual conversations. We've been talking to our home group ministry leaders, and they're going to incorporate a churchwide four-week seminar on recognizing God's fingerprints on your life story into their regular group gatherings. That's going to start after the community event. It's going to provide a great way for people inside and outside the church to consider God's claim on their lives. We think it's going to stimulate some great spiritual conversations about the six main things that we learned people are wondering about in their lives right now. So we're rewriting the scorecard for our outreach event. Instead of just focusing on the number of people who commit to Christ that night like we've done in the past, we're going to design it as a community-wide forum to start a conversation about life issues and spiritual questions. Our new goal will be to measure the number of new people at the event who we successfully escort into one of our groups based on personal invitations from their friends. That way, they'll be in a position to learn more about Christ based on life topics that interest them, and the people already in small groups will gain a built-in opportunity to have a spiritual conversation with the unchurched. Even better, these are life questions that even *our* people have told us they're curious to learn more about, so everyone will be on the journey together."

These are all just examples of ways you can use good information to set up a next move that your metapartners can facilitate with the people they lead . . . and they're moves based on needs those people *have actually expressed* on deepening the outcomes in their lives versus guessing or trying to talk them into something. Your partners will see real growth in people's lives when they're equipped with the right next step to offer the people they influence. If you're a church staff leader, you should wake up every morning and go to bed every night thinking, *How can I improve my system of ministry to better equip my partners with the right next move for their people?*

Step 5: EVALUATE: Assess Results to Plan Your Next Move

Once the move has been set up and implemented, the checkup loop isn't over. It's time to talk with your metapartners again at your next regular meeting. Here is where you find out how things worked, what changed, and what stayed the same. Best practices emerge from this conversation. Then, like Edison, your church leadership team retools again or scraps the idea or celebrates the win and determines the next area you want to focus on to research and improve to deepen the journey outcomes in people's lives.

Then, do it all again and again and again. That's what makes the checkup a *loop*. Your research once again comes from a refreshing combination of survey and dialogue, and can be as targeted or broad as needed based on the outcome(s) you choose to focus on. Whatever you do, engage over and over and over again with the people who are living with the plan and seeing firsthand what's happening in people.

Ministry like this isn't something you do on your own; it's a team sport. And not just within a specific ministry like groups or students or children's ministry or worship—I'm talking about the integrated whole of the church. To really close the awareness gap and the connectivity gap, you need all hands on deck to see the big picture and elevate the whole system. So in the next chapter, we'll look at how a leadership team operates day in and day out in a church with the kind of living, breathing, breakthrough ministry system we've been discussing.

CHAPTER 10

Operations Center: Building a Leadership Culture That Makes a Journey Seamless

I get to see a lot of different ministry strategies as I work with churches. As mentioned in an earlier chapter, one that I see frequently has three points. With variations here and there, it goes something like this: draw people into worship, cluster those people in smaller groups, and get them to serve somewhere to reach others. I've heard some say that this focus engages the heart, the mind, and the hands (or feet), respectively. In and of itself, it seems to be a reasonable strategy, but under it lurks the potential problem that it isn't personally owned by people across the entire church body.

A church I want to tell you about is one of these. This church—I'll call it Oakvale Church—has a special name for each part of their strategy: "God-Centered Worship," "Life Groups," and "Community Bridges." I find community bridges to be the most interesting part of this, because it takes a slant that you don't find in every church with a three-point strategy. In many churches, the third point involves serving, but it isn't well defined. It usually implies filling a volunteer role in various ministries of the church. In principle, service in such a church is intended to help the whole church draw more people in, but it often keeps the volunteer busier in the church rather than mobilizing them for life outside it.

Oakvale's community bridges weren't like this, though, at least on paper. For them, community bridges were mainly defined as a large number of activities that gave its people on-ramps to engage and serve the surrounding metropolitan area. The idea was that Oakvale's members would be ambassadors of the church and foster good will among those they served, leading to opportunities to share their faith. Oakvale ran and promoted a healthy variety of community bridges; life group leaders were expected to engage in them and get their groups to serve alongside them.

By the way, in the eyes of many evangelical leaders, Oakvale was a church to be admired and even emulated. As one of the largest congregations of its denomination nationally, the church had a number of vibrant missional initiatives. That rang especially true in Oakvale's passion for reaching its community—its neighbors—of 500,000 people with the gospel of Jesus. One of the church's values was "We love our community" and they meant it. The church was so committed to God's call to develop community bridges that its people gave millions of dollars to build a major regional community center for that very purpose. It was intended to be a hub for partnerships between Oakvale and other community entities— doing good *for* the community *with* the community. The church desired to do good works to build good will to share good news, as the lead pastor liked to say.

The community was amazed that a church would invest its own capital to build a facility as a gift to the community. And in just the first year, over a hundred thousand people were directly served by community center initiatives. By the numbers, it looked like an unqualified success, and Oakvale celebrated what God was doing. But the leaders of the church weren't satisfied to stop there and determined to dig more to continue furthering and deepening their reach. In part to find out whether the community center was truly facilitating daily community bridges in the lives of their people, the church broadly surveyed its regular attenders using specific journey outcomes and outcome expressions.

This is the story of what Oakvale's leaders found, what they did about it, and how they demonstrated a leadership culture that minds the gap.

Finding Gaps and Closing Them

The church's Mind the Gap Survey produced surprising and interesting results—some welcome and some very concerning.

Six particular statements on the survey had to do with respondents' engagement in community bridges—statements like "I regularly invite others to join me in community bridges" and "I strive to be an ambassador of good will for my church in the community." Not one of the six statements had a majority who said that it was often or always true of them. Only 1 percent of Oakvale's attendees said that all six described them often or always. Almost 90 percent said that at least half of the statements never, rarely, or only sometimes described them.

As I mentioned, even before the survey, Oakvale's leadership team was unsure about how many of their people were personally engaging in community bridges as a regular rhythm of their lives. The church taught about the importance of that idea a lot, but didn't truly know. The church staff and community partners were conducting a huge number of meaningful programs and church attendees would show up for many of them, especially bigger events with thousands of people, but leaders sensed their people's engagement was sporadic and might not be translating to daily missional living to the extent it could.

Still, they didn't expect these statistics. They could easily name many of the church's community bridges and the good things they were doing. They could recall exciting stories of how people grew in their relationship with Christ and how others came to faith in him through a community bridge. The leaders, of course, knew there was room to do more but still thought things were reasonably good.

It wasn't until they made a much broader effort to close their awareness gap that they realized the success stories described only a narrow minority of the church. Most people had little or no consistent involvement with this extremely important part of the church's strategy to reach its community. There was a significant amount of good activity going on, but not enough of Oakvale's people were engaged consistently in building relationships with non-Christians. Oakvale was doing good works and building good will, but its people were rarely sharing good news.

There were more concerning signs elsewhere in the survey. Another journey outcome had to do with caring for other people in one's neighborhood, workplace, and community. Oakvale's people were almost as disengaged from that habit of life as they were from community bridges. Another outcome involved having a spiritual influence on people who aren't yet followers of Christ. The same disengagement could be seen in that area as well.

The most telling survey results, however, had to do with the church's life groups. Responses revealed that a number of good things were happening in life groups: many people were learning, applying truth to their lives, sharing openly, and caring for others in their groups. At the same time, however, the survey revealed that most people's life groups weren't consistently serving the community together or helping participants find ways to build relationships with non-Christians.

In light of this data, Oakvale's leaders recognized at least two problems. One was a gaping connectivity gap between life groups and community bridges; people simply were not moving from one to the other. The other was an outcomes problem; whether in their church activity or their personal lives, most people were not engaging with non-Christians in a way that was likely to produce a gospel conversation or an invitation to church.

Oakvale is unique in many ways—every church is—but whether or not you can relate to some of their issues isn't the point. What I want you to see is how Oakvale responded within their missional calling and context. The leaders were rigorously intentional about grasping what was really going on underneath appearances, and repeatedly took thoughtful actions to change the reality.

The easiest, most simplistically minded thing you can do as a leader is to copy everything that I'm about to tell you Oakvale did. And that would be exactly the *opposite* of what Oakvale did.

Oakvale didn't copy anybody, because that's not how breakthrough systems are built. Don't copy what they did; copy how and why they did it.

On-the-Ground Metapartners Closed the Awareness Gap

Oakvale created a plan to engage their group leaders as metapartners much more deliberately. It began by convening life group leaders in groups and having open conversations about what they were seeing in their groups and in participants' lives.

They discovered several important things that were going on underneath the data. First, they found that many life group leaders had lost sight of their key role as the disciple-making hub of the church. A few years prior, there had been a big, successful drive to connect God-centered worship to life groups in creative ways, and a much larger percentage of worshippers engaged in life groups as a result. But amid the busyness generated by success, dialogue between life group leaders and staff had devolved into sporadic conversations about the next curriculum on the docket. As a result, the practical focus of life group leaders flattened from shepherding people comprehensively in the journey outcomes to managing content, care, and calendars.

Second, senior leaders learned that people in the church tended to participate in short-term projects, but they hadn't been converted to ongoing missional living. Indeed, there was a real possibility that many people didn't know the difference. If asked directly, they might recognize that they weren't involved in a community bridge consistently and weren't extending much spiritual influence or practical care to people outside the church. But apart from a direct challenge, many saw themselves to be engaged in their community because they served in occasional outreach initiatives from time to time.

Third, senior leaders tried to ascertain whether the survey results were pointing to something in the hearts of the people. Were people holding back from engaging with the community because they didn't care about lost people? Had the church grown inward and self-satisfied? Life group leaders didn't think so; they believed that most people knew they should make a genuine connection to share Christ with people, and they sincerely wanted to do so. But sociocultural pressures were clamming them up. They lived in a region of the country where being respectful about what you say and don't say so you don't rock the boat was deeply rooted in the culture. Many people in their city take a rationalistic approach to things, and people in the church felt unprepared to deal with skeptical questions or criticisms they might not know how to answer. It wasn't that people at Oakvale didn't care about their community— quite the opposite was true; they cared deeply. They just were balking at a chasm that they didn't know how to cross.

Next Moves Closed the Connectivity Gap

Next, after reestablishing a checkup loop with life group leaders, senior leaders experimented with ways to close the connectivity gap between their belief about God's desired outcomes and what people were experiencing through the church on their journeys.

Leaders realized that if people weren't evangelizing, it was going to be counterproductive to communicate to them that they were bad Christians. So they explored how to build a culture of evangelism to nurture its emergence and growth as a natural part of people's lives.

Keep in mind that they were looking to promote a defined journey outcome: having spiritual influence on those who aren't yet followers of Christ. It's not as if they hadn't tried to encourage people to engage with non-Christians before. They had done a lengthy sermon series on the topic, events, and an accompanying curriculum deployed through groups. As that initiative progressed, they had shining examples to spotlight of people sharing their faith and others coming to Christ. But the survey that was conducted later proved it hadn't actually changed the actions of *most* people in the church. It was as if they had prescribed medicine without thoroughly diagnosing the disease. They needed to do something different if they were to lead the bulk of the church to take a real step toward spiritually influencing others.

So, based on the results of the survey, this time they worked to set up a good series of next moves that people could handle and were likely to take. They started by looking more closely at trains that many people were already riding—worship gatherings and life groups. For a significant period, they started infusing into these constants a theme that they called bold faith moves. Over time, people were bathed in teaching that raised their awareness and cultivated their interest in taking a bigger than usual step of faith in their relationship with God.

These trains led up to a station that preachers and life group leaders were preparing people for: Go Bold Sunday. People came to worship that day knowing they would be challenged to commit to two bold faith moves of their choosing, one for spiritual growth (internal) and the other for spiritual influence (external). The bold moves people were asked to make, therefore, were actually commitments to a new train—whether an organized church ministry or a personal habit. Those new constants would lead people to grow in the outcomes of a Christlike, missional life.

People were free to commit to whatever bold faith moves they sensed God wanted them to take next. There was no comparison with anyone else as to whether the faith move was large or small; a move that might be easy to one person might require quite a lot of faith and boldness from someone else. To help people sort it out, however, each in-person and online attender was given information with several possible faith moves of each category. One of the possibilities for spiritual influence was *joining or starting a community bridge*.

At the Go Bold Sunday waypoint, half the attenders submitted a commitment stating their bold faith move—*with their name on it*. People were told in advance that the commitments would be read by senior leaders and then distributed to people's life group leaders. This would equip senior leaders' metapartners to carry on conversations with people in their groups about their bold faith moves. It was built-in accountability, but at the same time it wasn't putting anyone on the spot, because lots of people in the church were talking about their bold faith moves in this season. It also primed the checkup loop, because senior leaders could ask life group leaders about the progress and roadblocks they saw in people as they sought to live out their new commitments.

The commitment return laid the track for other moves. When senior leaders read over the commitments, they realized that people's faith moves could be clustered in categories. This allowed them to experiment with how to set up waypoints and constants to gather people with similar faith moves for extra encouragement, support, and instruction. The whole endeavor was so successful that Oakvale began working on creative ways to invite people to commit to two bold faith moves on an annual rhythm.

The bold faith moves initiative helped people start to cultivate a more missional daily lifestyle, but there was still more work to be done to bridge the gap between life groups and community bridge engagement. As a result of the feedback they received, leaders realized that there was a wide range of how people in the church were interpreting community bridges, some even feeling that a community bridge was simply inviting a friend to an event or serving or giving money to a short-term project at a local non-profit organization of their choice. These weren't necessarily *bad* things for people to do on their own, but they were outside of what leaders felt God was calling the church to focus on for community bridges in their context. So they realized a critical step would be to define and clarify to life group leaders and then to the rest of the church what a community bridge actually was:

> A community bridge naturally feeds into programming that's more connected to Oakvale Church;
>
> A community bridge gains significant goodwill, awareness, and brand recognition for Oakvale Church and/or the Oakvale Community Center;
>
> And most importantly, in a community bridge, Oakvale attendees and unchurched participants meet or deepen an existing relationship by regularly participating together.

The third part of the definition required the most clarification. Leaders spelled out repeatedly in multiple venues that volunteering at the city food bank (for example) was a wonderful thing to do to serve the community, but it was *not* a community bridge—unless, that is, you were consistently volunteering there with a group of people who weren't followers of Christ and building relationships with them over time through that involvement. This was a critical clarification for Oakvale's missional context and calling to use community bridges as a way for people to build relationships with non-Christians so they could ultimately share their faith.

Another step was to help people identify with a community bridge they'd be involved in. Leaders began by publicly defining two kinds of community bridges called church bridges and personal bridges. Both met all three of the criteria above. Church bridges were opportunities that, for the most part, already had been established and had some degree of recognition in the church as a ministry. Personal bridges, on the other hand, came out of an individual's or family's own initiative, something they were inclined to do that they could do with others. Leaders elevated both as legitimate options because they knew that some independent spirits wouldn't fit into the organization's mold but would want to do their own thing as a personal bridge, while others would be overwhelmed by the thought of creating or leading something new, but would become part of an ongoing church bridge that someone else was organizing.

The personal bridges that some people launched were diverse and creative. For example, a young married couple living in a university community loved independent films and decided to start a club. In no time, they had over twenty not-yet-Christians regularly joining them at their apartment to watch films and talk about how they relate to life and culture. The vast majority of the growing number of people coming continued to be non-Christians, giving the couple an opportunity to build relationships. The club let them talk openly about how their faith impacted their life and perspective on culture. It also gave them a natural way to demonstrate a glimpse of Christian community through their hospitality.

Another personal bridge was started by a guy who likes to ride his Harley-Davidson motorcycle. He started the Oakvale Rider Club for other motorcycle enthusiasts to go for a ride every Saturday morning. Some were believers and others weren't, but they consistently spent time together and talked about life.

Over an extended season of emphasis, Oakvale used multiple channels of communication. They communicated in public space by weaving the theme into sermons and social media. They communicated in personal space by reminding life group leaders to promote it. They also engaged a specialist to better communicate virtually and to integrate in-person and digital points of contact. They even began using a new term, *Good for All*, that better expanded and communicated deeper elements of neighboring and missional engagement.

As time passed, Oakvale's leaders listened repeatedly to their checkup loops and did follow-up mini-surveys to verify that their people really were moving toward defined outcomes. Not only were many more people engaged in a lifestyle of bridging relationships, a lot more connected the idea of *Good for All* to personal evangelism, which spilled into the rest of their lives. All this could happen because Oakvale reformed its leadership culture around knowing where people are and offering the right next moves based on people's progress toward outcomes on the journey together.

By the way, even while celebrating what God has done, Oakvale's leaders would be the first to tell you that they aren't finished yet. Like Edison, they realize they have more challenges to overcome and more exciting opportunities to improve that they continue to identify. All to consistently deepen their effectiveness at shepherding people toward God's destinations.

As part of their work, Oakvale focused on particular areas for improvement to emphasize over an extended season of six to twelve months. I like to think of this as an express train. In a rail system, an express train takes people from one point to another more quickly than usual because it skips some of the stops in between. This is not an exact parallel to my metaphor of trains and stations, but I still like the idea of an express train, because it represents a concerted effort to move people to a specific destination. It is a short-term area of focus that draws people's attention away from everything onto one thing in order to make a major advancement in that one thing.

A leadership team that continuously, rigorously closes the awareness gap can devise a sequence of express trains year upon year, one after the next, to move people further toward God's destinations according to their most pressing needs. But this can only happen in a leadership team that functions like an operations center.

How Teamwork Becomes More Than a Word on a Wall

Every rail system has an operations center that looks like pictures you've seen of NASA's mission control: ranks of desks with three monitors to a person and a huge video wall displaying feeds from all parts of the system, timetables, graphs, diagrams, and charts that make no sense to the untrained eye. On most days, the operations center is a fairly quiet, sparsely populated place with everything humming along as usual. But when there's an emergency like an extreme weather event, it becomes a beehive. A swarm of engineers and technicians rework the system on the fly to accommodate the disruption, to reschedule and reroute to get people where they need to go without a collision or a logjam at some part of the system.

Compare an operations center to your leadership team. Does your team operate with such knowledge of the situation on the ground, such a grasp of its ministry system, and such collaborative creativity that it can make agile adjustments in the moment that maximize the progress of people's journeys with God? In addition, unlike a rail system's operations center whose activity only peaks in an emergency, is your team working together in your church's operations center week in and week out?

Unfortunately, many more church leaders just say they value teamwork instead of actually operating like it. It's more typical to see ministry silos that don't act in concert with one another, to see individual leaders working as if they can succeed without or even at the expense of their colleagues, to see a lead or executive pastor act in an overbearing top-down way cloaked in the name of visionary leadership, or to see lay leaders appreciated as a workforce, as assistants, and as success stories but not as genuine partners mobilized around clear, integrated outcomes.

I'm also afraid that in many churches with impressive brain-power on its leadership team, the thinking machine isn't churning the right things. Some church staffs are very good at reading books to discuss over coffee—at least, I assume they're good at it, because they spend so much time on it. But they don't practice diligent, consistent investigation of what's really happening in the lives of the breadth of people in their church and experimenting with how to help them make their next right move with God based on defined journey outcomes. There is enough depth and complexity right under their noses to satisfy their minds' curiosity for years if they would only make the effort to consistently and intentionally look for it.

If you're a pastor, you can lead your team to be better than this, to genuinely resemble an operations center. It starts by repeatedly, relentlessly communicating messages such as:

- We never know as much about our whole church as we think we do.
- Our best stories are just one side of the story.
- Where are we leading by assumption?
- People will tell a survey and on-the-ground leaders things they'll never tell us.
- Facts are our friends.
- Focus not only on the message we state, but also the system we make.
- There can be no lazy shepherds.
- Don't spotlight, illuminate.
- Stop measuring success just inside our walls; measure how we're growing people's impact outside them.
- Are we making decisions based on the 10 percent we know about or the 90 percent we don't?

- Spotlighting is great for communication but terrible for overall evaluation.
- Are there any parts of our system that have become disconnected?
- Simple does not mean simple for us.
- Don't make God your excuse.
- Where are we being reactive instead of responsive?
- If people matter, our system that grows outcomes in their lives matters the most.
- Does this move the needle better than other things we could choose to do? How do we know?
- Have we checked up on this theory/plan with our metapartners?
- What lesser goals might be distracting us from God's best for us?
- Are our stations connecting people to our trains? How do we know?
- Are our trains taking people to our intended destinations? How do we know?

Messages like these continually impress the reality of the awareness gap and connectivity gap into leaders' consciousness. It reminds them that there is always more to know, that the most fascinating mysteries to explore are right in our own church, *and* that these mysteries really can be sleuthed out, not just shrugged off.

The early stages of defining outcomes and outcome expressions and creating a detailed outcomes-based survey make these messages real. The results validate that we always have areas of ignorance and a need for new knowledge. But they only make a team into an operations center or a laboratory performing breakthrough experiments when the results are received without blame. When they're accepted as realities, not judgments, they become the fun puzzle we get to solve together. Likewise, when we test something new with a portion of the church and check results through our checkup loop, we don't lay blame or get discouraged if it doesn't turn out as well as we might have thought. Failure isn't final. We celebrate with our leaders that we know something new about what *won't* work, which gets us closer to knowing what will. We fail faster so we succeed sooner.

The World's Most Interesting Meeting

You know the sort of meeting you dread the most because it's boring, uninformative, stale, or irrelevant to progress? Or busy, hamster-wheel-like, thrashing, and feels like survival mode? Or blame-laying, blame-shifting, uptight, and a minefield? A meeting in a church that's learned to mind the gap is none of these.

Instead, let me describe the sort of meeting you could lead in your church when you're building a culture of minding the gap.

First, the meeting I'm describing is attended by the lead pastor, plus an executive pastor or associate pastor if there is one, and the people overseeing each of the major ministry areas of the church.

The meeting begins with something similar to what Patrick Lencioni calls a *lightning round*.[1] In our case, each leader briefly shares one or two things happening in their ministry area that are

---

1. Patrick Lencioni, *Death by Meeting: A Leadership Fable* (San Francisco: Jossey-Bass, 2004), 146.

moving people toward a journey outcome or one of its expressions. One of those examples should pertain to the express train emphasis that the whole leadership group is focusing on at the time.

Remember, if we've named certain outcomes we're going for, our senior leaders have to be held accountable for how well their ministry areas are moving people closer to those destinations. This regular meeting is where you persistently redefine success, moving it from not just the number of participants in ministry activities but also—and more importantly—to the number of people progressing in journey outcomes.

After the lightning round, invite *one leader to present their area* in greater depth. (Leaders should get a heads-up to prepare before the meeting.) The leader gives more detail about what they've been learning and doing in their checkup loop with the metapartners in their ministry area. Based on that learning, they then share one specific thing they're wondering about or are considering researching further or trying next. That opens into a time of ideation with their colleagues for feedback and support in determining their next move.

Either the lightning round or the focus on one leader's area is likely to surface questions or issues that affect multiple ministries, even the whole church. The *checkup prioritization* that follows should allow the team to discuss and prioritize potential awareness gap and connectivity gap issues. This gives the team a chance to identify a specific topic for all leaders to take to their checkup loops or to start designing a plan for leaders and ministries to work together to move the needle on a particular outcome. It likely will yield a follow-up strategic meeting to flesh out options and decisions on a new direction.

The last element of the meeting is to discuss *task alignment*. The purpose is to clarify roles and assignments for next moves, including what should be communicated from leaders to each of their ministry areas in their weekly meeting. Even if an event or next move only directly pertains to one ministry area, there may well be important ways for other areas to cooperate by ensuring smooth connections between stations and trains.

The Fifth Layer: Learning Repeatedly

In the previous chapter, I introduced five layers of disciple moving—powerful parallels I see between moves management and disciple multiplication in the church. I described four of them: *leading deeply* into engagement and commitment, *knowing fully* what's going on in people's lives, *arranging wisely* people's next moves, and *partnering informatively* with others who are close to the people we want to guide to deeper commitment.

But there's one more layer: *learning repeatedly* by trying, checking, tweaking, and trying again, over and over and over.

We can always improve a bit more.

We can always close the awareness gap and the connectivity gap further.

We can always shepherd the flock, farm the field, and build the temple more effectively than we are today.

We can always engage with new people and new generations and new cultures more deeply with the life-transforming power of the gospel.

Life doesn't stand still; the world is always changing. So can we.

{ EPILOGUE }

The Voice in the Underground

In the first chapter of this book, I told of the origin of the memorable phrase "Mind the Gap," which booms over loudspeakers in stations of the London Underground so that passengers safely get on and off trains on the way to their destinations. That message and picture has been the theme of this whole book. But there remains one unusual story about one particular Underground station that has more to teach us.

Around 1970, a theater actor named Oswald Laurence stepped into a studio and recorded the words "mind the gap" for London Transport. He wasn't the first or the last to do it—over the years a number of people recorded the message, and at any given time a passenger could hear different recordings in different lines and stations throughout the system.

As stations were remodeled and recordings were updated, older ones were replaced. But Oswald's recording hung on for years at Embankment station, where four lines intersect in the heart of London—even after his death in 2007.

Oswald was survived by his wife, a general practitioner named Margaret McCollum. They met on a trip to Morocco in 1992—she was a tourist, and he had left the theater to work for a travel company. They married and spent the next fifteen years together. When Oswald died, Margaret was devastated. As she coped with her grief, she occasionally went to Embankment station to sit on a bench and listen to his voice. Even though he was gone, she felt closer to him there.

Then, on a November day in 2013, Margaret returned to Embankment station to hear Oswald's voice again, as she continued to do from time to time. But to her shock and sorrow, Oswald was gone. The recording had finally been replaced. It was almost as if he had died all over again.

Distraught, Margaret contacted the Underground's new administrative service, Transport for London, and inquired if there were any way she could get a recording of Oswald saying "mind the gap." Surprised but sympathetic, they made her a CD with Oswald's recording so that she could listen to him forever. Then they went a step further, reprogramming their new digital audio system so that Oswald Laurence would continue to tell passengers at Embankment station to mind the gap for years to come.[1]

When I think about Oswald and Margaret's story, I think about the countless voices shouting instructions at leaders through the loudspeakers of their lives every day. Through media old and new, by every possible channel, a deluge of ideas and techniques surges into leaders' ears, hearts, and minds, all in the name of helping them succeed in ministry.

---

1. "Mind the Gap Tube Announcement Returns after Wife's Plea," *BBC News*, March 9, 2013, https://www.bbc.com/news/uk-england-london-21719848.

And why not? There's a demand calling forth this supply. Whatever the size or life-stage of one's church—whether growing, plateaued, declining, or redeveloping—leaders of all kinds rightly feel that they need something more to see a multiplying harvest of maturing disciples. In a fast-paced culture of ever-increasing complexity, leaders are thirsty for true insight to cooperate with God to draw people to him and grow them in him.

Yet the effort to channel and filter all the voices can actually be counter-productive to making disciples. Applying what worked for someone else, somewhere else often doesn't work as advertised in one's own unique culture and context. And what seems like a fresh idea or perspective may not ultimately move people to a deeper place of personal engagement in Jesus's mission.

But if we listen closely, we can almost hear the Holy Spirit saying, "Mind the Gap." His voice is the supreme source of wisdom. His voice calls us to the stones we haven't turned over, the facts we haven't noticed, the data we haven't collected, and he tells us how to make sense of it. His voice speaks in the lively laboratory of leaders who try and test and try again and in the reports of metapartners who hear the hearts of the people.

There will always be a multitude of voices, some of them helpful. Still, nothing they say ultimately moves people to the places God wants them to go unless we attend to the voice of the Spirit as we mind the gap. Yet we have much reason to hope: if we do hear his voice and follow his guidance, many will find their spiritual journeys winding through our churches to God's destinations once more.